CLAMP

TRANSLATED AND ADAPTED BY

Anthony Gerard & William Flanagan

LETTERED BY

Dana Hayward

Tsubasa crosses over with *xxxHOLiC*. Although it isn't necessary to read *xxxHOLiC* to understand the events in *Tsubasa*, you'll get to see the same events from different perspectives if you read both!

Tsubasa Omnibus volume 1 is a work of fiction. Names, characters, places, and incidents are the products of the author's imagination or are used fictitiously. Any resemblance to actual events, locales, or persons, living or dead, is entirely coincidental.

A Kodansha Comics Trade Paperback Original.

Published in the United States by Kodansha Comics, an imprint of Kodansha USA Publishing, LLC, New York.

Publication rights for this English edition arranged through Kodansha Ltd., Tokyo.

First published in Japan in 2003 by Kodansha Ltd., Tokyo, as *Tsubasa*, volumes 1, 2 and 3.

ISBN 978-1-61262-595-9

Printed in the United States of America.

www.kodanshacomics.com

9 8 7 6 5 4 3 2

Translator: Anthony Gerard & William Flanagan
Lettering: Dana Hayward
Kodansha Comics edition cover design: Phil Balsman

Tsubasa Volume 1 Contents

Honorifics Explained

Throughout the Kodansha Comics books, you will find Japanese honorifics left intact in the translations. For those not familiar with how the Japanese use honorifics and, more important, how they differ from American honorifics, we present this brief overview.

Politeness has always been a critical facet of Japanese culture. Ever since the feudal era, when Japan was a highly stratified society, use of honorifics—which can be defined as polite speech that indicates relationship or status—has played an essential role in the Japanese language. When addressing someone in Japanese, an honorific usually takes the form of a suffix attached to one's name (example: "Asuna-san"), is used as a title at the end of one's name, or appears in place of the name itself (example: "Negi-sensei," or simply "Sensei!").

Honorifics can be expressions of respect or endearment. In the context of manga and anime, honorifics give insight into the nature of the relationship between characters. Many English translations leave out these important honorifics and therefore distort the feel of the original Japanese. Because Japanese honorifics contain nuances that English honorifics lack, it is our policy at Kodansha Comics not to translate them. Here, instead, is a guide to some of the honorifics you may encounter in Kodansha Comics books.

-san: This is the most common honorific and is equivalent to Mr., Miss, Ms., or Mrs. It is the all-purpose honorific and can be used in any situation where politeness is required.

-sama: This is one level higher than "-san" and is used to confer great respect.

-dono: This comes from the word "tono," which means "lord." It is an even higher level than "-sama" and confers utmost respect.

-kun: This suffix is used at the end of boys' names to express familiarity or endearment. It is also sometimes used by men among friends, or when addressing someone younger or of a lower station.

-chan: This is used to express endearment, mostly toward girls. It is also used for little boys, pets, and even among lovers. It gives a sense of childish cuteness.

Bozu: This is an informal way to refer to a boy, similar to the English terms "kid" and "squirt."

Sempai/
Senpai: This title suggests that the addressee is one's senior in a group or organization. It is most often used in a school setting, where underclassmen refer to their upperclassmen as "sempai." It can also be used in the workplace, such as when a newer employee addresses an employee who has seniority in the company.

Kohai: This is the opposite of "sempai" and is used toward underclassmen in school or newcomers in the workplace. It connotes that the addressee is of a lower station.

Sensei: Literally meaning "one who has come before," this title is used for teachers, doctors, or masters of any profession or art.

-[blank]: This is usually forgotten in these lists, but it is perhaps the most significant difference between Japanese and English. The lack of honorific means that the speaker has permission to address the person in a very intimate way. Usually, only family, spouses, or very close friends have this kind of permission. Known as yobisute, it can be gratifying when someone who has earned the intimacy starts to call one by one's name without an honorific. But when that intimacy hasn't been earned, it can be very insulting.

SAKURA!!!

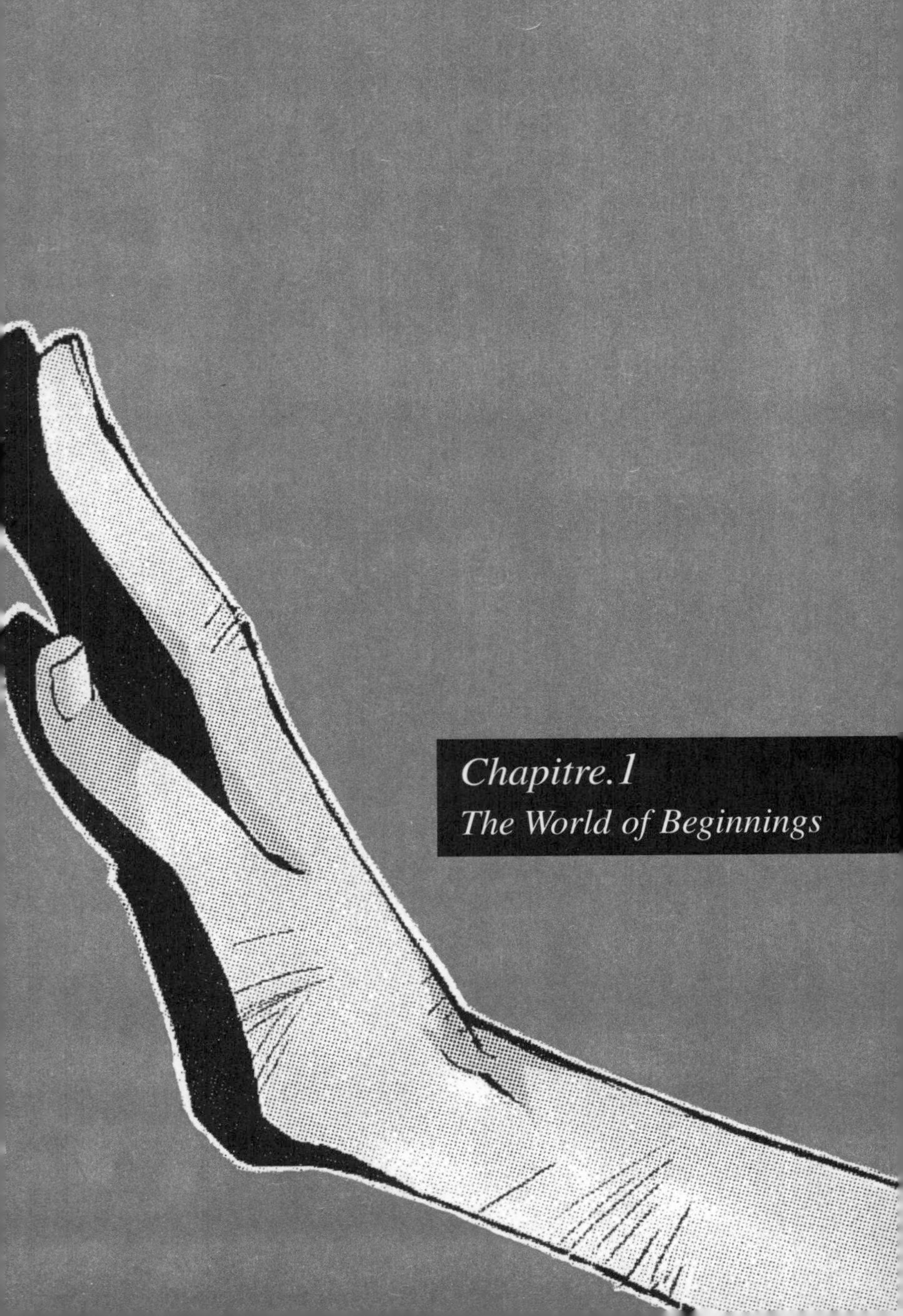

Chapitre.1
The World of Beginnings

RESERVoir CHRoNiCLE

TSUBASA

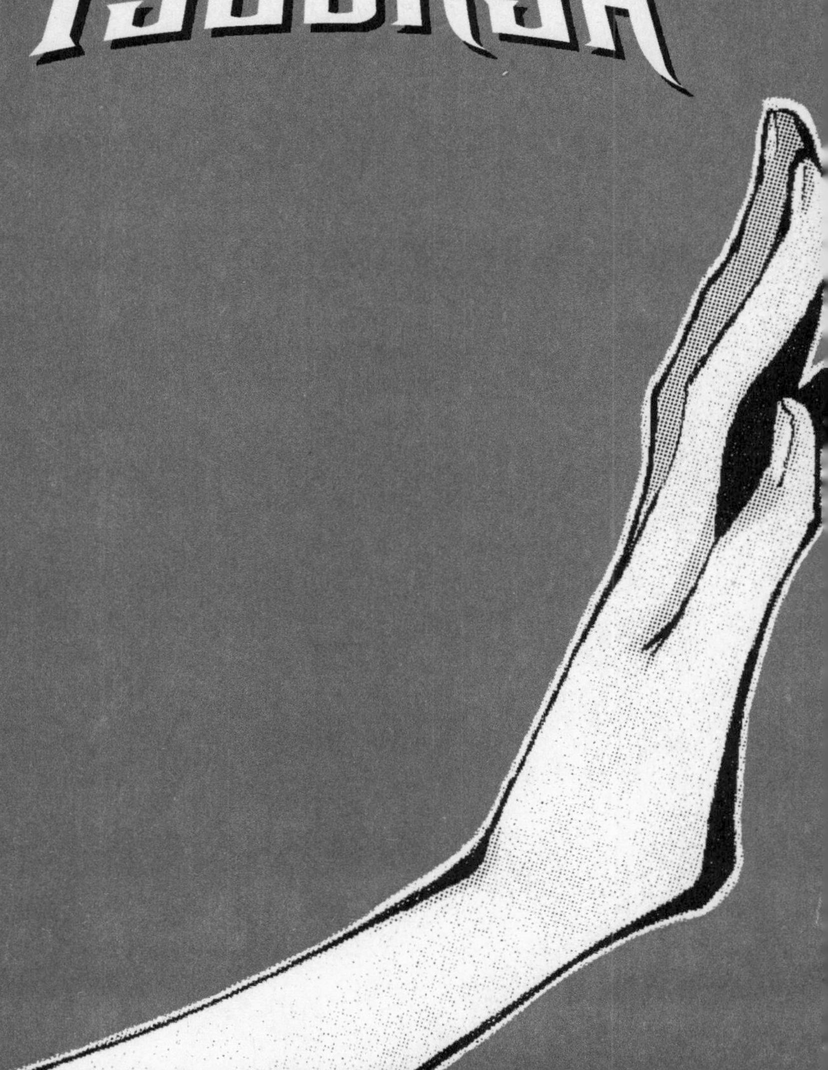

The Kingdom of
CLOW
KREE
TMP
TMP
THUMP
SHHK

SHUP
HELLO, FATHER ...
... I'M HOME.

YOU WERE RIGHT. IN THIS COUNTRY THE RUINS YOU SEE ARE ONLY THE TIP OF LARGER STRUCTURES BURIED IN THE SAND.
JUST LIKE YOU THEORIZED, FATHER.

BAM BAM
THE EXCAVATION OF THE EASTERN RUINS IS WELL UNDERWAY.

BAM BAM

KA-CHAK
YES?

SYAORAN!!
POFF
DONK
WAA!
WELCOME HOME! HOW WAS THE DIG AT THE RUINS? DID ANYBODY GET HURT? YOU DIDN'T GET A FEVER, DID YOU? HAVE YOU BEEN EATING PROPERLY?
Y— YES...
IT'S ALL FINE, YOUR HIGH-NESS.
I TOLD YOU...
...*NOT* TO CALL ME THAT!
HUMPH!
BUT...
...PRIN-CESS...
I TOLD YOU TO CALL ME *SAKURA!*
HUMPH! HUMPH!
YES, YOUR H—
NO! I-I MEAN...
O— OKAY.

BWIP
"SAKURA"!

S—
S— SAKURA.

HEH HEH HEH

GASP!
OH, I'M SORRY! I'M CUTTING OFF THE BLOOD TO YOUR LEGS!

CHIPOK

I'M REALLY HAPPY THAT YOU'RE HOME.
SYAORAN.
WHSPR
WHSPR
NICE TO BE BACK.

YOUR HIGHNESS KNEW—
SAKURA, YOU KNEW...
...WHEN I WOULD BE COMING BACK.

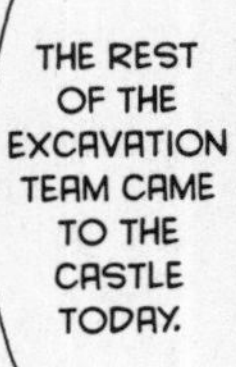
THE REST OF THE EXCAVATION TEAM CAME TO THE CASTLE TODAY.
TO REPORT ON THE SITUATION AT THE DIG.

AND YOU DON'T HAVE TO BE AT THE CASTLE NOW?

MY BIG BROTHER IS THE KING, AND *HE'S* THE ONE WHO HAS TO LISTEN TO REPORTS!

FWIP
AND IF THE EXCAVATION TEAM IS AT THE CASTLE...
...I WAS SURE THAT YOU WOULD BE COMING HOME!
BONG
YOU DIDN'T— YOU DIDN'T COME BY YOURSELF, DID YOU?

GLOOM
YUP!

AND WHEN I TOLD THEM THAT I WANTED TO SEE YOU...
...MY BROTHER GOT ALL GRUMPY, LIKE *ALWAYS!*
BUT WE GREW UP TOGETHER, AND I DON'T HAVE MANY DEAR, DEAR FRIENDS LIKE YOU!
RIGHT?

IT'S BEEN SEVEN YEARS, HUH?
SINCE YOU AND YOUR FATHER FIRST CAME TO OUR COUNTRY.
I'M STILL SURPRISED THAT AN INTERNATIONALLY FAMOUS ARCHAEOLOGIST LIKE YOUR FATHER WOULD BE INTERESTED IN CLOW'S RUINS.

HE TOLD US THAT THERE ARE PROBABLY RUINS BURIED BENEATH THE SANDS OF THE DESERT.
HE EXPLAINED TO THE PREVIOUS KING, MY FATHER, HOW WE COULD UNDERSTAND OUR COUNTRY'S HISTORY IF HE COULD BE ALLOWED TO EXCAVATE.
THE DESERT IS ALWAYS DANGEROUS, SO THE EXCAVATION TOOK CAREFUL PLANNING.
AND WHEN THE PREPARATIONS WERE FINALLY COMPLETE, THE DIGGING BEGAN.

HE DIED DURING THE DIG...
...BUT HIS LIFE WAS A HAPPY ONE.
HE WAS SMILING UNTIL THE END.

WE INVITED YOU TO COME LIVE WITH US WHEN HE PASSED AWAY!
WHY DIDN'T YOU?
I WOULD HAVE FELT WEIRD LIVING IN A CASTLE.
IT'S NOT WEIRD! AFTER ALL, WE'VE BEEN FRIENDS SINCE WE WERE KIDS!
YOU'RE ROYALTY! I'M A COMMONER!
COMMONERS CAN'T LIVE IN THE CASTLE!
BESIDES, I CAN AFFORD TO LIVE ON MY OWN WITH THE MONEY FROM THE DIG.
BUT...
GRMP

YOU'RE ALWAYS AT WORK. WE NEVER SEE EACH OTHER ANYMORE.
IT'S LONELY.
ISN'T IT LONELY FOR YOU?
IT'S LONELY.
BUT EXCAVATING THOSE RUINS WAS FOR BOTH ME AND MY DAD—
YES, I KNOW.
YOUR DEAREST DREAM.

I UNDER-STAND, BUT STILL...
...I MISS YOU WHEN YOU'RE GONE.
WHEN I'M IN THE CASTLE AT NIGHT... WHEN IT'S TIME FOR BED...
...I WONDER WHAT YOU'RE DOING AT THAT VERY MOMENT. I WONDER IF YOU EVER FIND TIME TO THINK OF ME A LITTLE.

I DO THINK OF YOU!
AND I WONDER, "WHAT'S SAKURA DOING NOW?"
UM... YOU KNOW, I...
I MEAN...
THERE'S SOME-THING I...
...WANTED TO...
...TELL...
...YOU.
?
WHAT IS IT?

UM...
UH...
I...
SYAORAN...
I LO–
BIIIING
BOOONG
UKK
GAMPH

BIIIING BOOONG
IT'S THE CASTLE BELLS.
I GUESS IT'S ALREADY EVENING
.....

B-BMP B-BMP B-BMP
B-BMP
ARE YOU ALL RIGHT?
UHHHHHHH.
JUST A LITTLE STARTLED.

I HAVE THE FEELING MY BROTHER SET OFF THE BELL ON PURPOSE!
SIGH
?
PURPOSE? WHAT PURPOSE?

NOTHING NOTHING
WHEN THE BELL RINGS, IT MEANS I HAVE TO GO HOME.
OR BIG BROTHER WILL BE HERE TO GET ME!
I'LL WALK YOU.
THAT'S OKAY! YOU MUST BE TIRED FROM ALL YOUR WORK! IT'S ALL RIGHT. I CAN GET BACK ALONE.

AND MY COUNTRY'S CITIZENS ARE ALL NICE PEOPLE!

THAT REALLY IS TRUE.
MY FATHER AND I TRAVELED TO ALL SORTS OF DIFFERENT COUNTRIES.
THIS IS THE MOST PEACEFUL COUNTRY WE'VE EVER BEEN TO.
THANKS!

UM...
YOU KNOW ...
THAT THING I WANTED TO TELL YOU?
WHEN WE MEET NEXT, I'LL TELL YOU THEN.
OH.
OKAY.
I *WILL* TELL YOU...
...SO WAIT A BIT.
OKAY?

TMP
YOUR HIGHNESS! GOOD EVENING!
TMP TMP
GOOD EVENING!
IT'S THE PRINCESS!
YOUR FACE LOOKS FLUSHED.
OH, IT'S NOTHING!
YOUR HIGHNESS, WOULD YOU HAVE AN APPLE?
THANK YOU! IT LOOKS DELICIOUS!
THESE EMOTIONS I'M FEELING...
...CAN NEVER BE.
RIGHT, FATHER?
WE MAY HAVE GROWN UP TOGETHER...
...BUT SHE'S STILL A PRINCESS.

TIP

そろ
TOE
そろ
TIP
GLANCE
GLANCE
そろ
TOE
そろ
TIP
そろ
TOE

YOU'VE BEEN SPOTTED...
SA
KU
RA!
KA SHAKK

DOOOM
I...
I'M HOME, KING TÔYA!
HI!
HAVE YOU BEEN WITH THAT HOLE-DIGGING TWERP AGAIN?
HE'S NOT A TWERP, AND HIS NAME IS SYAORAN!!
GRRR
TSK!
FOR A BRAT LIKE HIM, "TWERP" SUITS HIM JUST FINE!

HE'S NOT A BRAT EITHER! SYAORAN'S LIVING ON HIS OWN, AND DOING GOOD WORK! YOU SHOULD *RESPECT* HIM!
I WILL *NOT* RESPECT HIM! A BRAT'S A BRAT!
YAP
YAP
YAP
HE IS NOT !!
くすくす
PERHAPS WE SHOULD LEAVE IT AT THAT... YOUR MAJESTY...
YOUR HIGH-NESS ...
YUKITO-SAN!
HAVE YOU FINISHED YOUR PRIESTLY DUTIES?
TMP
TMP
YES.
WE KNEW OF THE ARRIVAL OF THE RUINS EXCAVATION TEAM AND THEIR REPORT.
AND HIS MAJESTY AND I AWAITED THEM HERE.

THEN TÔYA GOT SELFISH AND SKIPPED OUT, RIGHT?
NO, I'M NOT *YOU!*
ZHEEN
WHAT DID YOU SAY?!
HE LISTENED TO THEIR ENTIRE REPORT.
RIGHT THERE ON HIS THRONE
HUMPH
ZHEEN
THEY'VE COME A LONG WAY ON THE DIG.
IT SEEMS SO, YOUR HIGH-NESS.
FWAP
AND SOON THEY'LL FINISH DIGGING THE WHOLE THING UP!

NO.
IT LOOKS LIKE THERE IS MORE TO THESE RUINS THAN WHAT IS ABOVE GROUND.

WHAT?!
THEY'VE DISCOVERED A NEW UNDERGROUND PATH.
I DON'T KNOW HOW FAR IT'S GOING TO TAKE THEM, BUT I'VE GIVEN PERMISSION TO CONTINUE DIGGING.
AND SO...
THE EXCAVATION WILL GO ON.
AND THE TWERP WILL BE BUSY FOR A
LONG
LONG
LONG
LONG
TIME TO COME.
STAB
STAB
HEH HEH
GRND GRND

TH-THAT'S JUST FINE WITH ME!
EEEEE
SYAORAN'S JUST LIKE HIS FATHER! HE LOVES RUINS AND HISTORY AND STUFF LIKE THAT!
AND IF THERE'S SOME NEW RUIN, I'M SURE THAT'LL MAKE HIM THE HAPPIEST MAN ALIVE! SO IT'S *FINE WITH ME!!*

STOMP STOMP
YOU SHOULD NOT...
...PROVOKE HER SO, YOUR MAJESTY.
I TOLD YOU THAT WHEN WE'RE ALONE, YOU CAN DROP THE FORMALITIES.
YUKITO.
BUT...
TO THE PUBLIC WE MAY BE KING AND HIGH PRIEST...
...BUT WHEN THE JOB IS OVER, WE'RE JUST OLD FRIENDS.
YES, YOUR M—
AH!
OKAY.
HE JUST GETS ON MY NERVES.
THE LITTLE TWERP.

BUT YOUR SISTER, THE PRINCESS, IS SO CUTE, YOU JUST CAN'T HELP YOURSELF, CAN YOU?
AND TO THINK THAT SHE'S THE KINGDOM OF CLOW'S ONE-AND-ONLY PRINCESS AND THE FIRST IN LINE TO SUCCEED THE THRONE.

TRUE.
NORMALLY, ONE WOULDN'T EVEN BE ALLOWED TO *THINK* OF A COMMONER ASSOCIATING WITH ROYALTY.

BUT...
HE'S DESTINED FOR HER.
I'M RIGHT, AREN'T I?
ABOUT THAT?

YES.
SYAORAN IS...
...THE ONE PRINCESS SAKURA IS DESTINED FOR.

YOUR PREDICTIONS OF THE FUTURE ARE NEVER WRONG.
AND THAT'S WHY...

...IT *REALLY* GETS ON MY NERVES!
SHA POK

HOWEVER...

...THE TWO OF THEM HAVE ADVERSITY WAITING AHEAD.
ADVERSITY LIKE YOU'VE NEVER SEEN.

THE PRINCESS HAS AN UNUSUAL POWER.
I CAN'T SAY THAT I UNDER-STAND IT MYSELF.
BUT I *CAN* SAY...

...THAT IT CAN CHANGE THE WORLD.
IT'S THAT MUCH POWER.
AND THAT SAME POWER WILL BRING ON ADVERSITY.

YES, BUT IT WILL COME OUT ALL RIGHT IF WE'RE THERE TO HELP HER.
..... YES.

AND...
...EVEN IF WE AREN'T THERE...
...THE TWO OF THEM WILL COMBINE THEIR STRENGTHS TO FIGHT IT.

YEAH, BUT IT'S THE "TWO OF THEM" PART THAT I DON'T LIKE.
HUMPH
YOU NEVER GIVE UP...
...DO YOU, TÔYA?

STMP
STMP
HONESTLY !!
STMP

POMPH
MY BROTHER !!
HE NEVER STOPS TEASING ME!

SHF

KREEE
IT'S BEAUTIFUL.

AND BELOW IT, THERE'S SOMETHING MORE.

SYAORAN WILL BE SO HAPPY TO HEAR IT!
I'VE GOT AN IDEA! I'LL BRING LUNCH TO HIM TOMORROW! AND AT LUNCH-TIME WE CAN AT LEAST SPEND A LITTLE TIME TOGETHER!

THAT'S WHEN I'LL TELL HIM.

THAT I...
...LOVE HIM.

JIIING
EH?
JIIING

WHAT'S THAT SOUND?
IT'S PRETTY...
...AND A VERY CLEAR TONE.

A BELL?
JIIING
LIKE SOME-THING IS...
...BEING STRUCK.
IT SOUNDS LIKE IT'S COMING FROM THE RUINS.
JIIING
WHOOO
ALMOST LIKE IT'S...
...CALLING TO ME...

GASP
WHAT...
WHAT WAS THAT?
WAS THAT...
SYAORAN ?

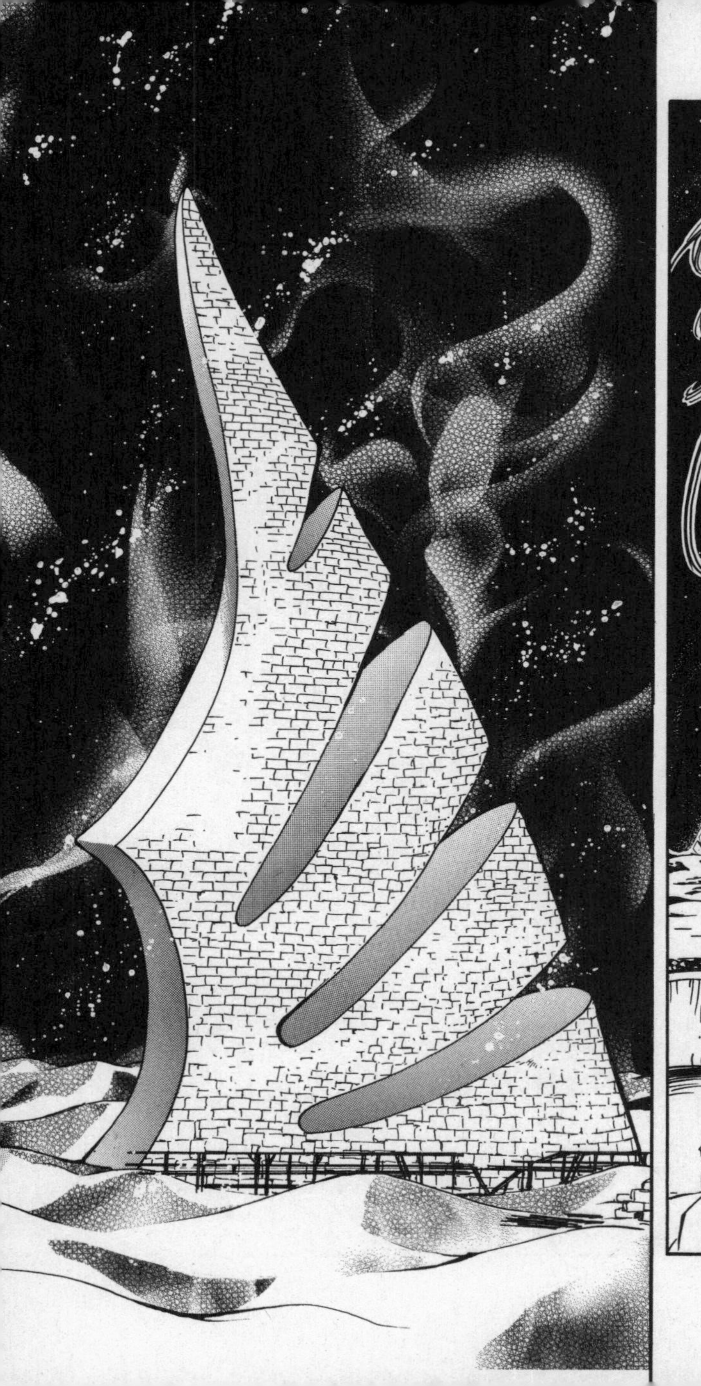

YADDA
YADDA
YADDA
YADDA
YADDA
YADDA
KANG
KANG
KATANG
KATANG
GASP
WHAT ARE THESE MARKINGS?
THEY'RE NOT FROM THIS COUNTRY'S HISTORY.
I'VE NEVER SEEN ANYTHING LIKE THEM BEFORE!
FLIP

HUHP
SYAORAN!
WAVE WAVE
WHAT IS IT?
I BROUGHT LUNCH FOR US! I ASKED SOMEBODY OUTSIDE, AND HE SAID THAT YOU WERE HERE!
DMP
IT'S DANGEROUS HERE!
THERE ARE NO REINFORCEMENTS OR SAFETY MEASURES. THE CEILING COULD FALL AT ANY TIME!
AND THE KING WILL BE WORRIED ABOUT YOU!
DON'T WORRY!
TÔYA'S HERE, TOO! HE'S ON AN INSPECTION OF THE SITE.
SST
HERE!

IT *LOOKED* LIKE IT WAS AN UNDER-GROUND PASSAGE ...
...BUT IT CAME TO A DEAD END HERE.
IT'S MADE OF SOME INCREDIBLY STRONG ROCK. WE'VE TRIED EVERYTHING, BUT WE CAN'T GET BEYOND IT.
THIS HERE ...
I SAW IT LAST NIGHT.
EH?

PAA AAA
ZZZ
ZZZ
PAKAH
ZZZ
PAKAH
GWOOM
WHAT'S GOING ON?
ZZZ
ZZZ
ZZZ

PAAAAA
SSSS
SAKURA!!
RRMM
MM
WHAT'S GOING ON?
MM
IS IT AN EARTH-QUAKE ?
AAAAHH!
AAAHH!
IT'S BREAKING UP! GET AWAY!
MM
MM

NO! THIS IS NO EARTH-QUAKE!
KREE EEE
SHDDA SHDA
KRAKK
AAARG!
SLSS
ZZZ
THERE'S SOMETHING GOING ON BELOW!
AAH! AAAAHH! AAH!
WHERE DID THESE MEN COME FROM?!
SSHINGG
DOON

SAKURA!
TMP
TMP
TMP
TMP
TMP
TMP
TMP
WHAT IN THE—

SAKURA
!
SAKURA
!!
KAK
WHAT'S GOING-?!
VWAAAAA

THE POWER TO PASS THROUGH SPACE AND TIME...

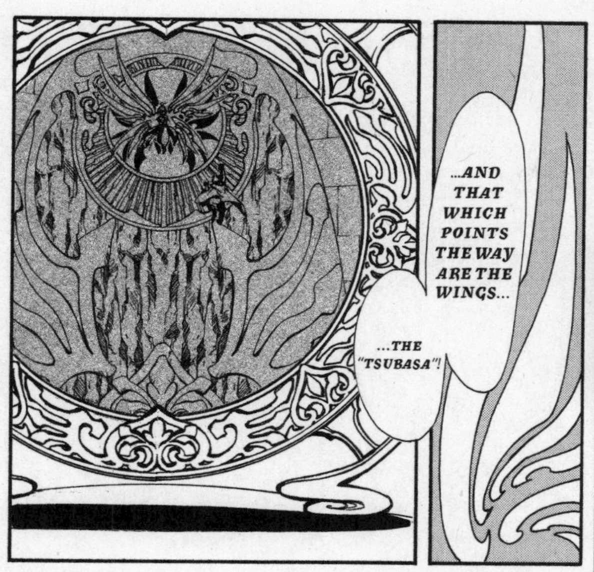
...AND THAT WHICH POINTS THE WAY ARE THE WINGS...
...THE "TSUBASA"!

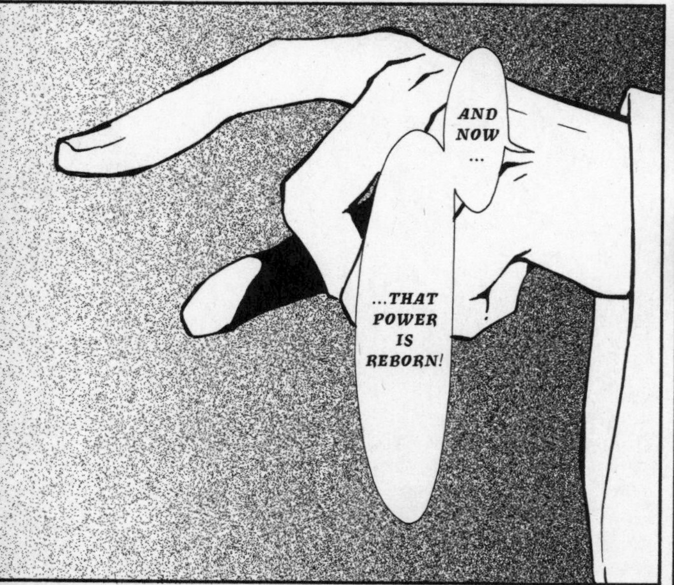
AND NOW...
...THAT POWER IS REBORN!

GRMP
SLOOO
SLOOO
SLOOO
DMP
SAKURA!!
VAAM
SLOOOOM

BOK
KRASSH
ZYOON
ZYOON
JIIIING
KRAKL
RRRMMBBL
KRAKL
ZYOON
ZYOON

RRRRRM
SAKURA!
SAKURA!!
SHE'S GETTING COLDER AND COLDER!
I HAVE TO GET HER OUTSIDE!
MMMMMBBL
IT DIDN'T WORK, DID IT?

PERHAPS, BUT THIS IS THE BEGINNING.

AND WHEN IT'S DONE...
...I WILL HAVE...
... A POWER THAT SPANS UNIVERSES!

SHFF
WHAT HAPPENED?!
HEH
YOU'RE LATE, TWERP.
YOU BETTER NOT HAVE LET SAKURA GET HURT!
SHOOM
YOUR MAJESTY!!
THDD
HE WAS HIT WITH THE POISONED TIP OF AN ENEMY ARROW!
WILL HE BE ALL RIGHT?

I WILL *NEVER* ALLOW HIM TO DIE!

THE PRINCESS!!
GASP
THERE WAS A STRANGE RELIEF BELOW IN THE RUINS...

SST

I'VE READ YOUR MEMORY.

THE PRINCESS'S WINGS HAVE TAKEN FLIGHT.
WHAT?

ZZZT
THE WINGS AND THE PRINCESS'S HEART ARE ONE.
HER... HEART?
ALL OF THE PRINCESS'S MEMORIES FROM THE MOMENT OF HER BIRTH TO NOW HAVE VANISHED.
AND . . .
. . .HER HEART IS NOWHERE TO BE FOUND ON THIS WORLD!
HOW CAN THAT—

WITHOUT HER HEART, HER BODY IS NOTHING MORE THAN AN EMPTY SHELL.
SHE CAN'T STAY THIS WAY...
...OR SHE'LL...
IS THERE SOME-THING I CAN *DO* FOR HER?
ANY-THING?!
KLNCH
THERE ISN'T A MOMENT TO LOSE!
AND I'LL TAKE RESPONSI-BILITY FOR WHAT HAPPENS!
SHLOO
LOO
SHLOO
I WILL SEND YOU TO SEE SOMEONE IN ANOTHER WORLD.
SOMEONE WHO, LIKE ME, CARRIES THE POWER OF THE MOON.

WHO IS THAT PERSON? WHAT SHOULD I DO WHEN WE MEET?
PAAAAAAA
SHE IS CALLED THE *SPACE-TIME WITCH!*
YOU WILL TELL HER EVERYTHING, AND...

GWAAAA
YOU WILL BEG HER TO HELP THE PRINCESS!

GWABOH
KLNCH
KEEE
SAKURA!!
GRM
GRM
GRM
GRM
EEE
EEE

DWOOM

SHHH
HH
HH
HHH
ARE YOU...
ARE YOU THE SPACE-TIME WITCH?
I HAVE BEEN CALLED THAT.

WOULD YOU PLEASE...
I NEED YOU TO SAVE SAKURA!!

ツバサ
RESERVoir CHRoNiCLE

Chapitre.2
The Price of Memory

The Country of
JAPAN

AHH HA HA HA HA! WEAK! WEAK! YOU'RE ALL *WEAK!!*

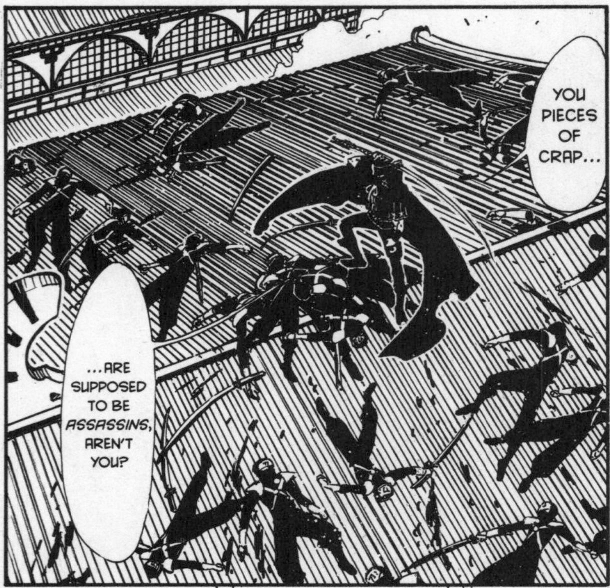
YOU PIECES OF CRAP...
...ARE SUPPOSED TO BE *ASSASSINS*, AREN'T YOU?

CAN'T YOU SEND ANYONE WITH *GUTS* TO FIGHT ME?
あー?!
COME ON!
ONCE AGAIN YOU DIDN'T DO WHAT I ASKED, DID YOU...
... KUROGANE?
CHING
PRIN-CESS?
TMP
DON
EVERY IMPUDENT SLOB WHO TRIED TO SNEAK INTO SHIRASAKI CASTLE HAS BEEN TAKEN CARE OF! HOW CAN YOU HAVE A COM-PLAINT ABOUT THAT?

I ASKED YOU TO AVOID UNNECESSARY DEATH...
...WEREN'T THOSE MY WORDS?
TMP TMP
KYAAH! KYAAH!
TAKKA TAKKA
ONE OF THE FIRST RULES FOR NINJA IS TO CUT DOWN THOSE WHO ATTACK YOU, PRINCESS TOMOYO.
I HAVE NEVER HEARD SUCH A RULE.
AAAAAAH!
CAN'T YOU JUST SHUT UP?
KUROGANE! HOW CAN YOU BE SO RUDE TO HER HIGH-NESS?!
NO, DON'T BOTHER, SÔMA.
GUESS THERE HAVE TO BE GOOD ONES AND BAD ONES.
SIGH
WITH SUCH LOYAL, GOOD NINJA AS SÔMA, WHY ARE THERE ALSO SUCH NINJA AS YOU, KUROGANE?
HEH!

LOOK, I WANT TO BE BETTER THAN I AM!
I WANT TO BE THE *BEST!!*
THAT'S WHY I FIGHT!
AND IF MY ENEMY LIVES OR DIES IN THE PROCESS, IT'S NOT *MY* WORRY!

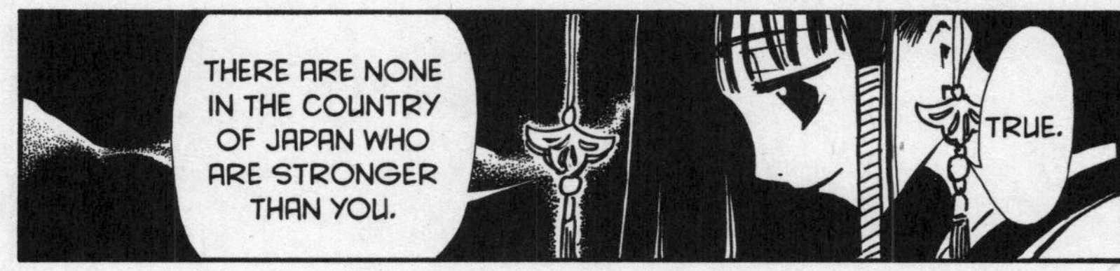
TRUE.
THERE ARE NONE IN THE COUNTRY OF JAPAN WHO ARE STRONGER THAN YOU.

SO...WE HAVE NO CHOICE LEFT.
SST

EH?

WHAT'S GOING ON?

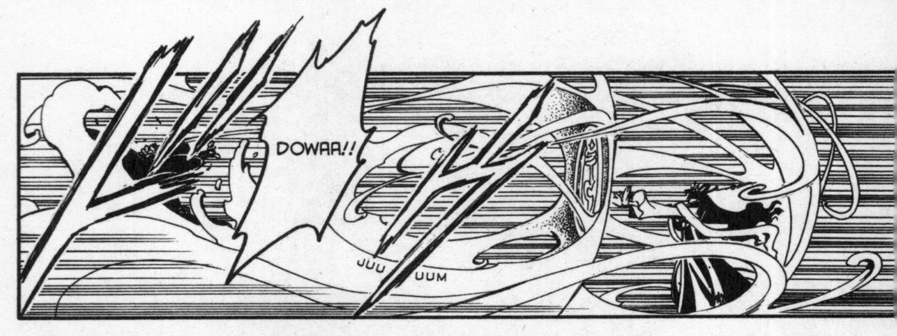
DOWAA!!
JUU UUM

IN THE OLD DAYS, THEY ALWAYS SAID THAT THE BAD ONES MUST JOURNEY TO GET BETTER.
HO HO HO
THEY NEVER SAID THAT!!

SO NOW I'LL SEND YOU FLYING TO ANOTHER WORLD.
ZUBOK
UGAAA
I DON'T WANT TO FLY!!
ZUBOK

YOU WILL MEET A GREAT MANY NEW PEOPLE.
IT IS THERE THAT YOU WILL LEARN THE TRUE MEANING OF STRENGTH.

AND TO THAT END...
ALTHOUGH IT PAINS ME GREATLY, I WILL SEE YOU OFF.
VSSH
ZUBOK
ZUBOK
YOU'RE NOT SEEING ME OFF, YOU'RE *FORCING* ME OFF!
AH, I NEARLY FORGOT.
YOU REQUIRE ONE LAST USE OF MY ARTS.
POP
ZLUUU
PAA
AAA
WHAT THE HELL IS *THIS!*

A CURSE.
FROM THIS MOMENT ON, UNNECESSARY DEATH WILL BE FORBIDDEN TO YOU.
FOR EACH PERSON YOU KILL, YOUR STRENGTH WILL LESSEN. I SUGGEST YOU TAKE CARE.

CUT THIS OUT, TOMOYO!
GWAAA
FARE-WELL.
HO HO HO HO
AND IF FATE ALLOWS IT, WE'LL MEET AGAIN.
TSK TSK
HOW DARE YOU ADDRESS HER HIGH-NESS THAT WAY?

ZUBOK
ZUBOK
PLEASE BE WELL ON YOUR JOURNEY...
...KURO-GANE!

I'LL BE BACK, AND DON'T YOU FORGET IT!!
ZU BOPH

DO LOPP
YOUR HIGHNESS... UMM...
KUROGANE...
HIS JOURNEY...
I SENT HIM TO "THAT PERSON." I'M SURE A GOOD FUTURE WILL BE ARRANGED FOR HIM.
...HAS JUST BEGUN.

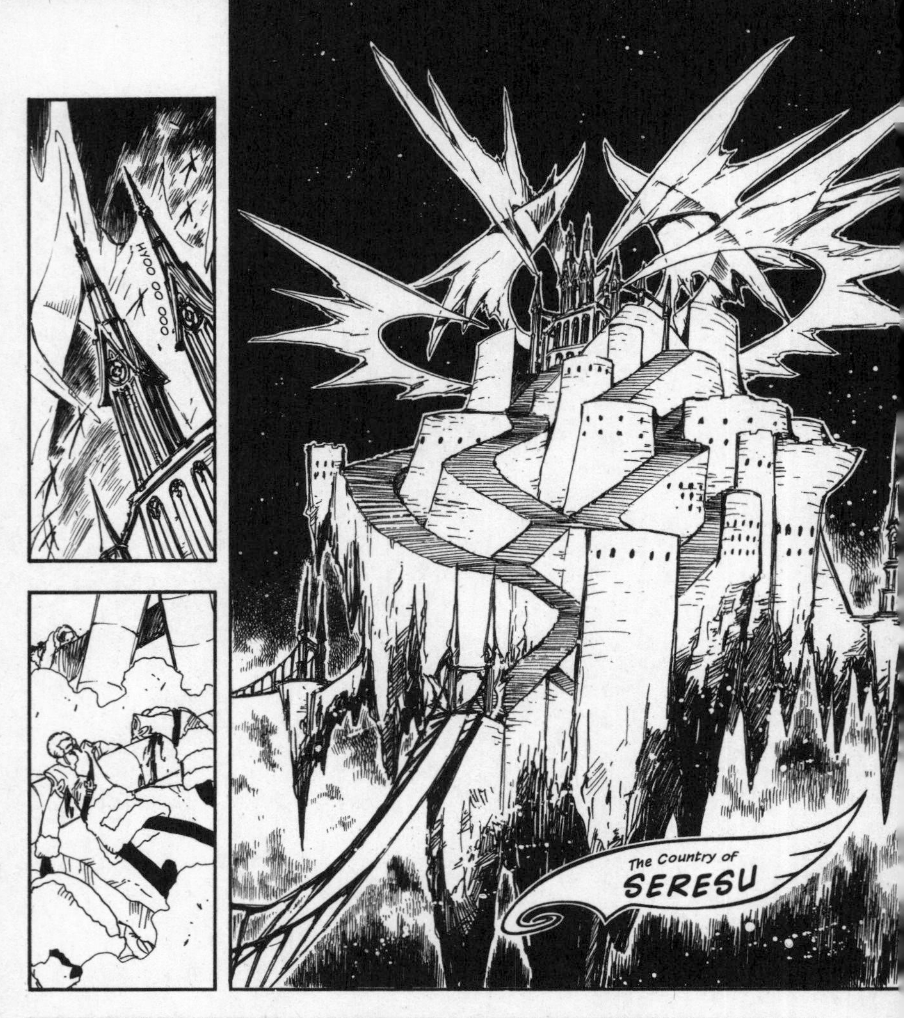
HYOO OO OOO
The Country of
SERESU

ZYOOM
GATCH

SU PASH

DID YOU SLEEP?
MY KING?

FFSSH

YES.
THIS IS THE ONLY WAY I CAN.
WHAT WILL YOU DO NOW...
...FAI?
I CAN'T STAY IN THIS COUNTRY ANY LONGER.

MAYBE ...
...NOT EVEN THIS WORLD...
... HUH?
WORLD?
I MEAN THIS DIMENSION.
I STILL DON'T UNDER-STAND.
MMMM.
GOOD CHI
GOOD CHI
FOR *YOU*, CHI...
... THAT'S ALL RIGHT.

WHOOPS. I'M ALMOST OUT OF TIME.

WHOOSH
CHI?
I HAVE TO BE ON MY WAY.
TO WHERE?

VERY FAR AWAY.
AS FAR AWAY AS I CAN GET.
SOME PLACE WITH NO KING ASHURA.

BUT I HAVE A FAVOR TO ASK OF YOU, CHI.
WHAT IS IT?

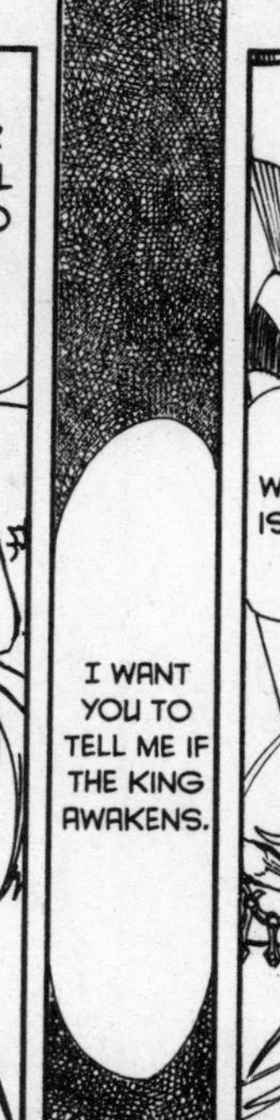
I WANT YOU TO TELL ME IF THE KING AWAKENS.

SO I WONDER IF IT'S ALL RIGHT TO CHANGE YOU A LITTLE.
IT'S JUST FINE.

AFTER ALL, FAI *MADE* CHI!

PAAA AAA

PAAAAAAAAAA

AT LEAST ...
WHILE YOU'RE ASLEEP, HAVE *GOOD* DREAMS!

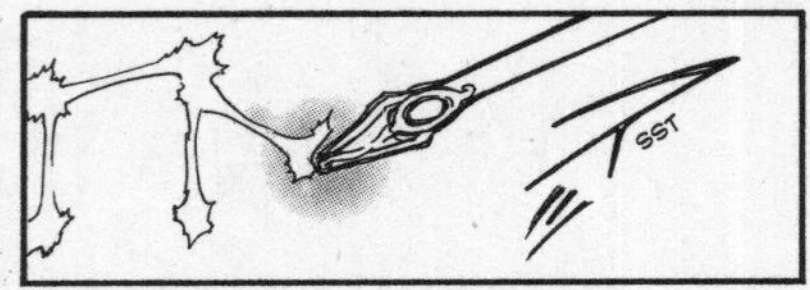
SST

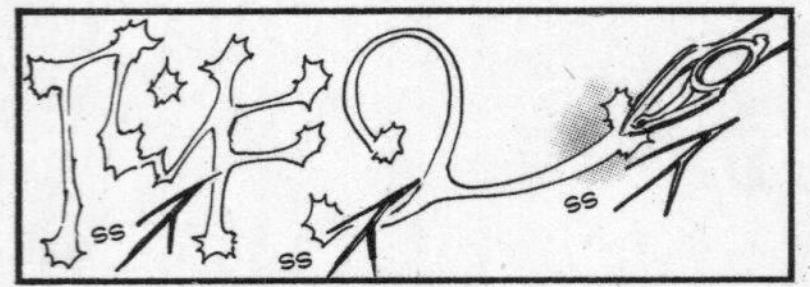
SS
SS
SS

ALL RIGHT!
FWOOON

TIME TO GO...
GLOOB

...TO SEE THE WITCH!

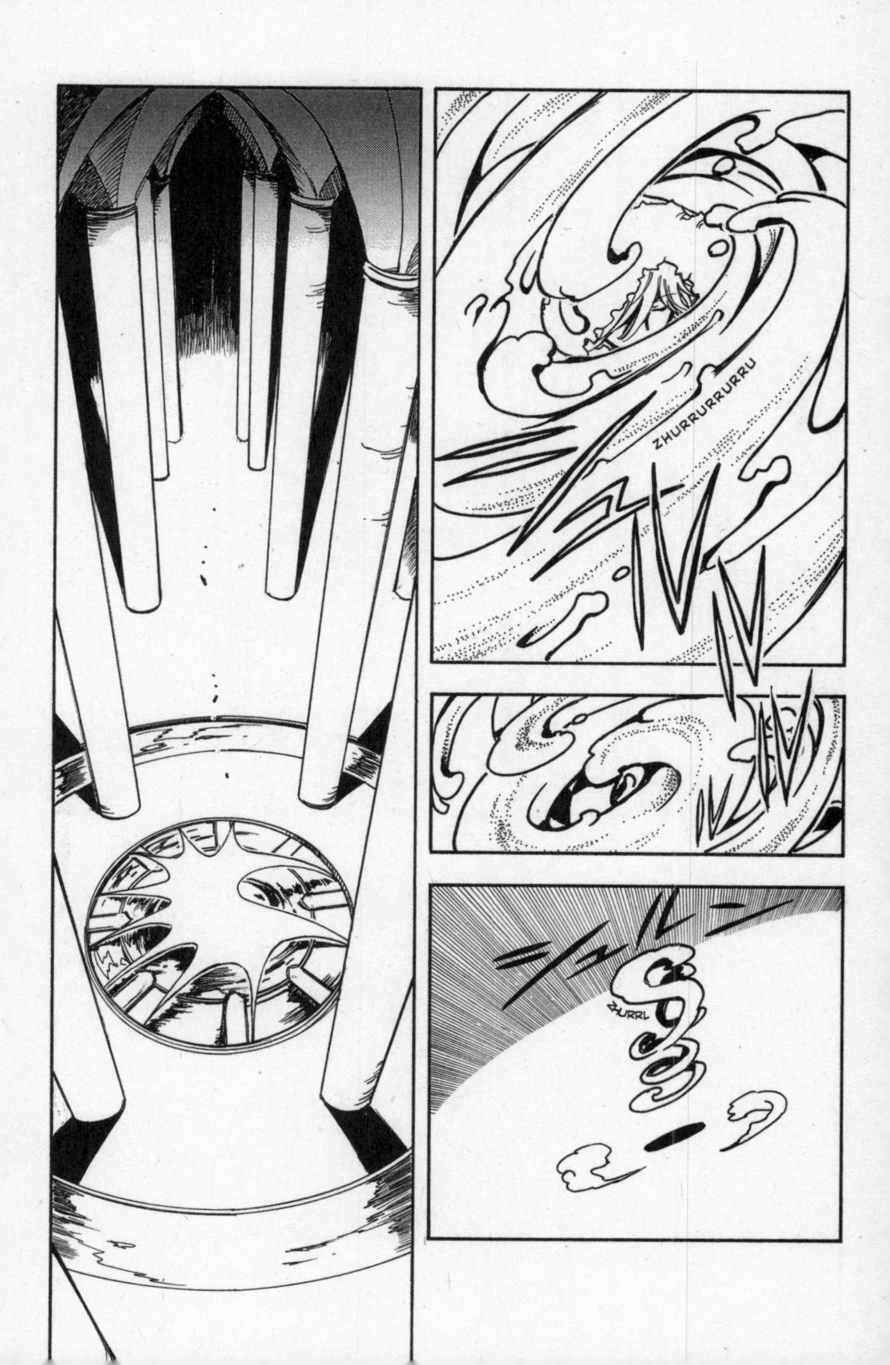
ZHURRURRURRU
ZHURRL

SHHH
HHH
HHH
THIS CHILD'S NAME IS SAKURA, ISN'T IT?
AND YOU?
YES!
I'M SYAORAN.
SST

THIS CHILD...
...HAS LOST SOME-THING VERY PRECIOUS.
...YES.

AND...
...THAT SOMETHING HAS BEEN SCATTERED TO MANY DIFFERENT WORLDS.
IF NOTHING IS DONE...
...THIS CHILD WILL DIE.
GIISH

WATANUKI?
Y— YES?
GO TO OUR TREASURE ROOM. THERE IS SOMETHING I NEED YOU TO BRING BACK.

YOU WISH TO SAVE THIS CHILD?
AH!
UM ...
ER...
TMP TMP TMP TMP
YES!!

THERE *IS* A PRICE.
ARE YOU STILL WILLING?

I WILL PAY *ANY* PRICE I CAN!

KEEEEEEE
GASP

EEE
HERE THEY COME.
EEE
EEE
EEE

ARE YOU THE DIMENSION WITCH?
WHO THE HELL ARE YOU?
WHAAA?
EH HEH

GRR

PLEASE GIVE ME YOUR NAMES FIRST.

ME? I'M KUROGANE.
I MEAN...
...WHAT *IS* THIS PLACE?
WHAT ARE THESE WEIRD BUILDINGS ALL AROUND?
IT'S CALLED JAPAN.

EH?
MY COUNTRY'S CALLED JAPAN, TOO.
YES. A DIFFERENT JAPAN.
I'M NOT GETTING ANY OF THIS!
NOT ONE BIT!

AND YOU?

SHT
THE WIZARD OF SERESU.
FAI D. FLOWRIGHT.
DO YOU KNOW WHERE YOU ARE?

YES...
A PLACE WHERE ANY WISH CAN BE GRANTED IF A SUITABLE PRICE IS PAID.
THAT'S EXACTLY IT.

AND SO...
...THE REASON WHY ALL OF YOU ARE HERE...
...IS BECAUSE EACH OF YOU HAS A WISH.

MY HOME WORLD...
...IS WHERE I WANT TO BE!
...IS THE PLACE I DO *NOT* WANT TO BE.

STARE
THAT IS A TALL ORDER...
...FOR BOTH OF YOU.
NO...

...FOR ALL *THREE* OF YOU...
... PERHAPS.

EVEN IF YOU OFFERED THE MOST PRECIOUS THINGS YOU OWN, NONE OF YOU HAS ENOUGH TO PAY...

... BUT ...
...IF ALL THREE PAID TOGETHER, YOU MAY JUST BE ABLE TO AFFORD IT.

WHAT KIND OF *CRAP* ARE YOU SPOUTING?
MR. BLACK, CAN YOU KEEP YOUR INSULTS DOWN?
HEY!

I'M *NOT* "MR. BLACK"!
I'M KUROGANE!!

ALL THREE OF YOUR WISHES ARE THE SAME.

YOU WANT TO GO TO MANY WORLDS IN ORDER TO RESTORE THE MEMORY OF THIS CHILD.

YOU WANT TO RETURN TO YOUR OWN WORLD.

YOU WANT TO GO TO DIFFERENT WORLDS TO AVOID RETURNING TO YOUR OWN.

YOU HAVE DIFFERENT REASONS, BUT THE METHOD IS THE SAME.
TRAVEL TO DIFFERENT DIMENSIONS ...THAT IS WHAT YOU NEED.
EACH OF YOU INDIVIDUALLY CANNOT MAKE THAT WISH HAPPEN.
HOWEVER, IF THE THREE OF YOU COMBINE PAYMENT FOR ONE WISH, THEN YOU CAN AFFORD IT.
THEN WHAT WOULD *MY* PAYMENT BE?
YOUR SWORD.
WHA- ?!
GAK
I'D *NEVER* GIVE YOU GINRYÛ!

FINE!
ZMM
INSTEAD YOU WILL WANDER THIS WORLD LOOKING LIKE A COSTUME-CONTEST LOSER, AND GET PICKED UP BY THE POLICE FOR CARRYING AN UNLAWFUL SWORD, AND GET PLASTERED ALL OVER THE TV FOR BEING A FREAK! IS THAT WHAT YOU WANT?
ZMM
HUH?
POLEE?
TIIVII?
ZMM

YOU REALIZE THAT YOU ARE TRAPPED HERE, AND I AM THE ONLY PERSON IN THE WORLD WHO CAN GET YOU OUT?
THAT'S *GOT* TO BE A LIE!!

TWIK
IT'S ALL TRUE.

YOU'RE KIDDING!
EH HEH HEH

WHAT WILL YOU DO?

CHNK
DAMMIT!!
VAK
WHEN I AM FREE FROM THIS *CURSE*, I AM COMING BACK FOR IT!

YOUR PRICE...
...IS YOUR MARKING.

I DON'T SUPPOSE THIS STAFF WOULD DO INSTEAD?
I TOLD YOU, THE PRICE IS THE THING YOU VALUE MOST.
FSH
IT WON'T.
ZUUU
I GUESS I HAVE NO CHOICE.

WHAT ABOUT YOU?
NOW IS THE TIME TO HAND OVER YOUR ITEM OF HIGHEST VALUE.

AND YOU WILL BE ABLE TO TRAVEL THE WORLDS.

FINE!

YOU REALIZE THAT I HAVEN'T NAMED THE PRICE YET.
YES!

THE ONLY THING I CAN DO IS SEND YOU TO OTHER WORLDS.
FINDING THE CHILD'S MEMORIES IS SOMETHING *YOU* WILL HAVE TO DO.

.....
FINE!

I LIKE YOUR ATTITUDE.
TMP TMP
EH?
THERE'S MORE OF YOU.
HERE THEY ARE.
SST

THE NAME OF THIS YOUNG ONE IS MOKONA MODOKI.
MOKONA WILL LEAD YOU THROUGH THE WORLDS.
FWISH

HEY, YOU GOT AN EXTRA. GIVE IT TO ME.
I'LL GO HOME WITH THAT.

NO. THAT'S HOW WE KEEP IN CONTACT.
SEE HOW USE-FUL?
TSK!
THE ONLY POWER THIS ONE HAS IS TO STAY IN COMMUNICA-TION WITH MOKONA.

MOKONA WILL TAKE YOU TO DIFFERENT DIMENSIONS, BUT THERE IS NO WAY TO CONTROL WHICH DIMENSION.
FOR THAT REASON, ONLY FATE WILL DECIDE WHEN YOUR WISHES WILL BE GRANTED.

HOWEVER, THERE IS NO COINCIDENCE IN THE WORLD.
WHAT IS THERE IS "HITSUZEN."
AND WHAT BROUGHT YOU TOGETHER...
...WAS ALSO "HITSUZEN."
SYAORAN...
...YOUR PRICE IS...
...YOUR RELATION-SHIP.

THE THING YOU VALUE THE MOST...
...IS YOUR RELATIONSHIP WITH HER.
SO THAT IS YOUR PRICE.
MY PRICE? BUT HOW–
EVEN IF...
...THIS CHILD'S MEMORIES ARE COMPLETELY RESTORED...
...YOUR RELATIONSHIP WITH HER WILL NEVER BE THE SAME AGAIN.

SO WHAT IS SHE...
...TO YOU?
A CHILDHOOD FRIEND ...
...AND THE PRINCESS OF A COUNTRY ...
... AND ...
...AND A GIRL WHO IS PRECIOUS TO ME!
GRMP

HOW-EVER ...
...IF YOU WANT TO ACCEPT MOKONA, THAT RELATION-SHIP WILL END.
..... I SEE.
EVEN IF YOU RETRIEVE ALL OF HER MEMORIES ...
...THE ONE MEMORY THAT YOU WILL NEVER RETRIEVE WILL BE HER MEMORY OF YOU.
THAT IS MY PRICE.
WILL YOU STILL PAY IT?

LET'S GO.
I WILL *NOT* LET SAKURA DIE!

Chapitre.3
The Wings of Hitsuzen

TRAVEL BETWEEN WORLDS IS MORE DIFFICULT THAN YOU IMAGINE.

THERE ARE A WIDE VARIETY OF WORLDS.
FOR EXAMPLE ...

THE WORLDS THESE TWO COME FROM.

YOU CAN TELL JUST FROM THEIR CLOTHES, CAN'T YOU?
BOTH OF THEM COME FROM DIFFERENT WORLDS THAN YOURS.

PEOPLE YOU KNOW. PEOPLE YOU'VE MET ON YOUR WORLD...
...THEY'VE DEVELOPED UNDER COMPLETELY DIFFERENT CONDITIONS ON OTHER WORLDS.
YOU MAY MEET DIFFERENT VERSIONS OF THE SAME PERSON TIME AFTER TIME ON DIFFERENT WORLDS.
AND JUST BECAUSE THAT PERSON IS NICE TO YOU ON ONE WORLD DOESN'T MEAN YOU WILL FIND AN ALLY ON THE NEXT.
YOU'LL FIND WORLDS WHERE YOU CAN'T COMMUNI-CATE—WHERE EVEN COMMON SENSE DOESN'T WORK.
SCIENTIFIC DEVELOP-MENT, STANDARD OF LIVING, LAWS...ALL CHANGE WITH THE WORLD.
THERE ARE WORLDS FULL OF CRIMINALS, WORLDS OF LIARS, WORLDS LOCKED IN CONSTANT WARS...
AND YOU MUST LIVE THROUGH THEM ALL.
IT WILL BE A JOURNEY IN WHICH YOU WON'T KNOW WHERE YOU ARE NOR HOW CLOSE YOU ARE TO COLLECTING ALL OF THE FRACTURED PIECES OF MEMORY.

THAT SAID ...
...ARE YOU STILL DETERMINED TO SEE IT THROUGH?
.....
YES!
SINCERITY AND DETERMI-NATION...
NO MATTER WHAT A PERSON WANTS TO ATTEMPT, THOSE ARE NEEDED.
AND IT SEEMS THAT YOU ARE WELL PROVIDED WITH BOTH.
WOOOOOOOOO
AND SO ...
PAKEEEEEN

PAAAAA
YOU MAY GO!
GWAA AHH

FSSH
GOWAAAAAAA
GASP

PAKUNG
SHU
LOOM
PISH
PISH
FFWAA
PLIP
I WISH...

...YOU THREE THE BEST OF FORTUNE ON YOUR JOURNEY!

SAKURA...
SHE'S THE MOST PRECIOUS PERSON TO ME!
SHE'LL ALWAYS STAY THAT WAY!
AND SO...

NO MATTER WHAT HAPPENS TO US. NO MATTER WHAT WE DO! I WILL NOT LET SAKURA DIE!
EVEN IF IT MEANS THAT SAKURA WILL FORGET ME!
I'LL NEVER ...
SAKURA!!

PUU!
IT LOOKS LIKE...!
SA...
...KURA?
BLINK
GASP
GAMPH
SAKURA!
...HE DOESN'T PLAY ALONG WITH MOKONA!
SNIFF SNIFF
WOBBL
HUP
OH!
IT LOOKS LIKE HE'S UP.

GRMP
WE TRIED TO DRY HER OFF.
SHE GOT PRETTY WET IN THE RAIN.
MOKONA DRIED, TOO!
EVEN WHILE YOU SLEPT, YOU WOULDN'T LET THE GIRL GO.
SO YOU...
ER...
えへー
えへー
SEE? SEE?
ほめてー
PRAISE ME!
CALL ME SYAORAN.

MY NAME IS PRETTY LONG.
YOU CAN JUST CALL ME FAI.
BOING

AND...
...MR. BLACK OVER THERE. WHAT'LL WE CALL YOU?
I AM *NOT* "MR. BLACK"!
BOING

I AM KUROGANE!

KUROGANE, HUH?
ほいほい
GOT IT
SO WHAT WORKS? KURO-CHAN? KURORIN?
HEY!
YOU... THING! DON'T GET COMFORTABLE THERE!
POFF

HER BODY...
...IS LIKE *ICE!*

SHE CAN'T STAY THIS WAY!
BEFORE WE START LOOKING FOR HER MEMORIES...
...WE HAVE TO HELP SAKURA!

ZWOOP
WAA!!
ごそごそ
RUSTLE
RUSTLE
HMMMM.
WHAT DO YOU THINK YOU'RE DOING?!
SHFF
SHFF
IS THIS WHAT A PIECE OF MEMORY LOOKS LIKE...
...FOR THIS CHILD?
SII IP
EH?!
IT WAS STUCK TO YOU.
ONLY ONE, THOUGH.
BOING

THAT TIME WHEN ALL THE FEATHERS FLEW AWAY!
WAFF
THIS...
...IS ONE PIECE OF SAKURA'S MEMORIES!
SST

HER BODY ...
...IS A LITTLE WARMER.
HAH
IF YOU HADN'T HAD THAT FEATHER, IT MIGHT HAVE BEEN A PROBLEM.
EH
HEH
BY COINCIDENCE, ONE STUCK TO MY CLOTHES...
THERE IS NO COINCIDENCE IN THE WORLD.

THAT'S ...
...WHAT THE WITCH SAID, WASN'T IT?
AND SO...
...MY GUESS IS WITHOUT THINKING, YOU GRABBED IT YOURSELF.
BYUUN
IN ORDER TO SAVE THE GIRL.
OF COURSE, I'M JUST GUESSING ALL THIS!
EH?
SLUMP
.....
BUT MY QUESTION IS, HOW CAN WE FIND THEM NOW...
...HOW CAN WE FIND NEW FEATHERS?
I DOUBT WE'LL FIND ANY MORE IN OUR CLOTHES.
MUDGE MUDGE

はーーい はいはい
MEEEEE! MEE! ME!
MOKONA KNOWS!!

HUH?
BOING
THAT FEATHER GAVE OUT *REALLY* BIG WAVES!

SO WHEN A FEATHER IS CLOSE, MOKONA WILL FEEL THE BIG WAVES!
TWRL
TWRL

AND MOKONA WILL BE LIKE...
BWAHH
GAK!
...THIS!!

WELL, IT LOOKS LIKE WE HAVE A WAY.
IF WE GET CLOSE, MOKONA WILL LET US KNOW.
PAT
PAT
PAT
B-BUMP B-BUMP
WOULD YOU DO THAT? TELL US WHEN WE'RE NEAR A FEATHER?
LEAVE THAT TO ME!!
TA-DAAH
THAP
THANK YOU!
SEARCH OR DON'T SEARCH. THAT'S UP TO YOU.
IT'S GOT NOTHING TO DO WITH ME!

I'M HERE TO GET BACK TO MY OWN WORLD.
THAT'S THE ONLY REASON I'M HERE.
DON'T EXPECT ME TO STICK MY NECK OUT FOR YOU. DON'T EXPECT ME TO HELP YOU.
I WON'T DO IT!

NOD
RIGHT.
THAT IS *MY* MISSION HERE.
I'LL DO MY BEST NOT TO CAUSE YOU ANY TROUBLE.

HA HA HA HA HA!
SYAORAN, YOU ARE SO *SERIOUS!*
?
TCH!

MM?
ARE YOU GOING TO HELP THE BRAT OUT?
HMMMM.
I SUPPOSE SO.
WELL? WHAT ABOUT YOU?
MY MOST IMPORTANT MISSION IS TO *NOT* RETURN TO MY WORLD.
SO, IF IT DOESN'T THREATEN MY LIFE... SURE, I'LL HELP OUT.
GAK!
HI!
I'VE GOT NOTHING BETTER TO DO.

GASP
KA-CHAK
YO!
KA-KLAK
SO YOU'RE ALL AWAKE NOW!
HEY! NO NEED TO GET ALL TENSE!
YOU CAME FROM YÛKO-SAN, RIGHT?
TM
TM
YÛKO-SAN?
YOU KNOW, THE GIRL WITCH.
THE DIMENSION WITCH . . . THE FAR EAST WITCH . . . SHE HAS A LOT OF NAMES.

HERE.
OH! THANK YOU!

I'M SORATA ARISUGAWA.

BOW
I'M ARASHI.

JUST TO LET YOU KNOW, SHE'S MY WIFE AND THE WOMAN I LOVE.
I CALL HER MY "HONEY"!
無視
NOT LISTENING
ヒョイ
HEFT
JUST MAKE SURE YOU'VE BURNED THAT INTO YOUR HEARTS.

BY WHICH I MEAN THAT IF YOU LAY A FINGER ON HER, YOU'LL DIE HORRIBLY. ♡
POFF
TWRL

WHAT BLISS I FEEL HAVING A HONEY LIKE THIS!
AHHH...
HERE.
I'M SYAO-RAN.
BOW

WHY DO YOU SAY THAT ONLY TO *ME*?!
NORI! IS LIFE!
NORI! NORI!
あははは
AH HA HA HA

BUT I WASN'T KIDDING!
いい笑顔
BRIGHT SMILEY FACE
HUP
I WON'T TOUCH HER!!

HYOI
NOW...
I FIGURE YOU WENT TO THE WITCH LADY, AND GOT
THIS
FROM HER TO GET HERE, RIGHT?
TA-DAH
MOKONA MODOKI!

THAT'S A LONG NAME.
IS IT OKAY IF I JUST SAY MOKONA?
SURE!
OKAY!

I HEARD THE WHOLE STORY FROM THE MAN THERE.
I MEAN THE BLONDE GUY.
MR. BLACK OVER THERE IS TOO MEAN TO ASK!
SHUT UP!
EH HEH

ANYWAY, GENTLE-MEN . . .
THIS IS YOUR LUCKY DAY.
UMM . . .

IN WHAT WAY?

MOKONA HAS NO IDEA WHICH IS THE NEXT WORLD, RIGHT?
STMP
STMP
SO . . .
. . . IT'S A HAPPY CHANCE THAT BROUGHT YOU TO THIS WORLD FIRST OF ALL.

BECAUSE THIS . . .
SHOOO

...IS THE HANSHIN REPUBLIC!
のみだおれ
HANSIN

ツバサ
RESERVoir CHRoNiCLE

Chapitre.4
The Strength to Fight

THIS IS THE HANSHIN REPUBLIC.
THE BEST OF ISLAND NATIONS.
WE ARE SURROUNDED BY SEAS ON ALL SIDES. WE GET THE ODD HURRICANE, BUT WE HARDLY EVER HAVE EARTHQUAKES . . .
WE HAVE SEVERAL TRADING PARTNERS ACROSS THE SEAS, AND WE EXPORT LIKE CRAZY!
WE HAVE FOUR SEASONS.
RIGHT NOW, WE'RE IN FALL.
THE SEASON WHERE RICE TASTES ITS BEST!
SPRING GREAT FLOWER VIEWING!
SUMMER SEASON FOR BEER!
FALL RICE TASTES ITS BEST!
WINTER BEST SEASON FOR NABE!
THE MAIN STAPLE IS WHEAT FLOUR.
AND OUR SAUCE IS FAMOUS!
TIGER SAUCE
KLIK
WE HAVE THE HANSHIN REPUBLIC CONSTITUTION AND RULE OF LAW!
FWIK
AND BY LAW, WE NEVER MAKE WAR WITH OTHER COUNTRIES.
MODES OF TRANSPORT . . .
. . . CAR . . .
. . . BICYCLE . . .
. . . MOTOR-CYCLE . . .
. . . TRAIN . . .
. . . BOAT . . .
. . . PLANE . . .
. . . AND ONE COULD CONSIDER A *BABY CARRIAGE* TO BE ONE FORM OF TRANSPORT, RIGHT, HONEY?
. . . . .

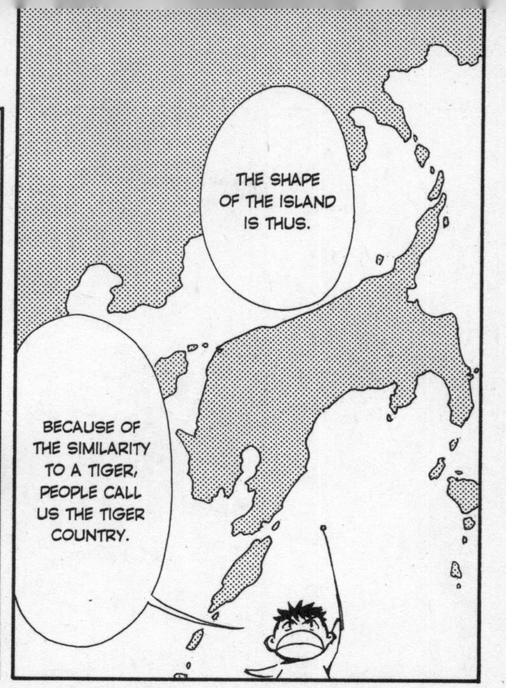
THE SHAPE OF THE ISLAND IS THUS.
BECAUSE OF THE SIMILARITY TO A TIGER, PEOPLE CALL US THE TIGER COUNTRY.

OF COURSE, THE HANSHIN REPUBLIC USES THE IMAGE OF A TIGER QUITE A BIT.
OUR CURRENCY IS THE KOKO. (TIGER)
THERE ARE ONE-KOKO COINS, 100,000 KOKO BILLS, AND THE TIGER HEAD IS THE SYMBOL OF THE COUNTRY.

.....
AND THE LOGO FOR OUR BASEBALL TEAM IS THE SAME!

THIS YEAR, THE TEAM HAS SOME REALLY GREAT PROSPECTS!
SOME OF THE BEST PLAYERS IN THE WORLD!
BUT THE TEAM'S A ROUGH & TUMBLE GROUP OUTSIDE THE PARK!

SIR!
I HAVE A QUESTION!

YES?
FAI-KUN?
VIP
DOES EVERYONE IN THIS COUNTRY HAVE AN ACCENT LIKE YOURS, SORATA-SAN?
BASEBALL? WHAT THE HELL IS THAT?

AWW, DON'T BE SO FORMAL! CALL ME SORA-CHAN!
SORA-CHAN?
OKAAAY!
OKAAAY!
......
MY ACCENT IS UNIQUE TO ME. IT'S AN OLDER VERSION OF OUR LANGUAGE.

YOURS IS A LANGUAGE THAT THEY USED IN THE PAST?

THAT'S RIGHT!
NOWADAYS HARDLY ANYONE USES THIS LANGUAGE.
I'M A HISTORY TEACHER, AND I'M FIRMLY AGAINST ALLOWING ALL THE OLD WAYS TO FADE AWAY.
春
BOING
YOU'RE A HISTORY TEACHER?

おう!
I AM!
I TAKE IT YOU HAVE AN INTEREST IN HISTORY?
YES!
IN MY WORLD, I USED TO WORK ON ARCHAEO-LOGICAL DIGS.
THEN I'D SAY WE HAVE SOMETHING IN COMMON!

AND I HAVE ONE MORE QUES-TION!
はーい
MEEE!
はーい
MEEE!

NOW ...
EXACTLY WHERE ARE WE? WHO OWNS THIS ROOM?
GOOD QUESTION!
THIS IS AN EMPTY ROOM IN AN OLD, TRADITIONAL APARTMENT HOUSE THAT MY HONEY AND I MANAGE.
GAMPH
......
AIN'T IT GREAT?
A BEAUTIFUL APARTMENT MANAGER WHO IS ALSO A GREAT COOK!
WAY OUT OF IT
うっとり…

YOU! WAKE UP!!
SHOOM
PA KOW
WHAT WAS THAT?
HOOSH

I DIDN'T FEEL AN ENEMY! WHO DID THAT?
GLANCE GLANCE
きょろきょろ
BASTARD! *YOU* THREW THAT, DIDN'T YOU?

YOU WERE IN A CORNER. IF HE THREW ANYTHING, IT WOULDN'T HIT YOU THERE.
IT HAD TO COME FROM ABOVE.
WHAT?
IT WAS MY *KUDAN*, WHAT ELSE?

"KUDAN"?

YOU DON'T KNOW?
SURE YOU DON'T!
YOU ALL COME FROM DIFFERENT WORLDS! YOU *WOULDN'T* KNOW!

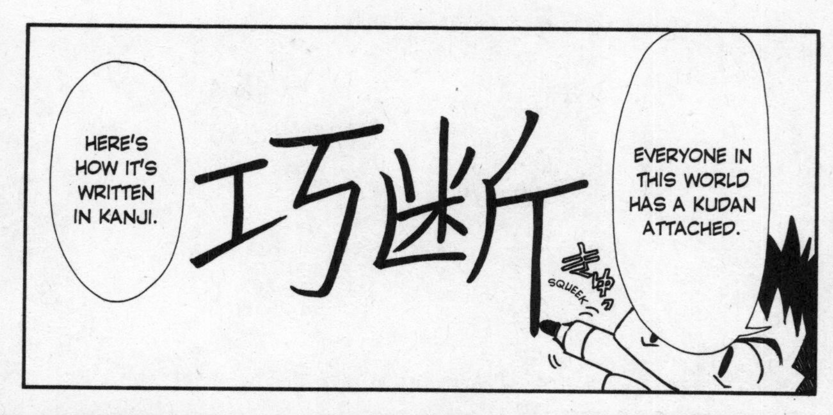

KUROGANE AND SYAORAN'S WORLDS USE KANJI, BUT FAI'S PROBABLY DOESN'T.

BUT YOU CAN UNDERSTAND WHAT I SAY, AND I UNDERSTAND YOU.

HMM. HMM.

あははは

AH HA HA HA HA

きゅっ

POK

NOW...
WHAT KIND OF TECHNIQUE IS THIS KUDAN?
AND YOU USED THE WORD... ATTACHED.
EVEN IF YOU COME FROM ANOTHER WORLD, ONCE YOU ENTERED THIS ONE, A KUDAN WILL BE ATTACHED.
DO YOU MIND IF I CALL HER SAKURA-SAN?
THAT'S FINE.
SST

I CANNOT SAY WHERE SAKURA-SAN'S MEMORY WENT...
...HOW-EVER, IF SOMEONE HAS PICKED IT UP...
...IT WILL BECOME THE CAUSE OF A FIGHT.
YOU'VE LOST YOUR METHOD OF BATTLE.
HOW DID YOU KNOW?
MY HONEY USED TO BE A SHINTO RELIGION MIKO.
SHE POSSESSES SPIRITUAL POWERS.

WELL ...
FYUU
SHE'S RETIRED EVER SINCE SHE MARRIED ME.

HER BEAUTY WHEN SHE WAS DRESSED AS MIKO WAS A GOD-SEND!
SIZZL
もえもえや~
SIZZL
HEH HEH HEH
NOT LISTENING
無視

EH HEH
ACTUALLY ...
I DID GIVE MY MAGIC POWER TO THE DIMENSION WITCH.

AND I HANDED MY SWORD TO THAT BITCH!

IT WASN'T ANY SORT OF POWER THAT I GAVE HER.
I NEVER HAD MAGIC OR WEAPONS OR ANYTHING LIKE THAT FROM THE START.

THAT MAY HAVE BEEN YOUR GOOD LUCK.
EH?

THERE ARE KUDAN IN THIS WORLD.
WHEN IT COMES TIME TO FIGHT, THAT KUDAN SHOULD BE ABLE TO HELP.

THEN THIS KUDAN WAS ORIGINALLY MEANT FOR BATTLE?

WHAT YOU USE IT FOR...
...OR HOW YOU USE IT IS ALL UP TO YOU.
HEH
ONE LOOK CAN ANSWER A HUNDRED QUESTIONS.
IF YOU WANT TO SEE WHAT YOUR KUDAN IS...
...THE ONLY THING TO DO IS SEE IT WITH YOUR OWN EYES.

NOW...
...I'VE PRETTY MUCH EXPLAINED EVERYTHING TO KNOW ABOUT THIS COUNTRY.
NOD NOD
HE DID?

HM?
WELL?
WHAT DO YOU THINK?
DO YOU THINK THAT SAKURA-CHAN WOULD HAVE A FEATHER ON THIS WORLD?

.....
SURE DOES!

IT IS STILL A LONG, LONG WAY AWAY, BUT...
...THIS COUNTRY HAS ONE.

SHALL WE FIND...
...THIS FEATHER OF YOURS?
YES!
AND YOU MEN, DO YOU FEEL THE SAME?

I MIGHT AS WELL.

NO!
MOKONA ...
...WILL NOT LEAVE THIS COUNTRY UNTIL MOKONA FINDS THE FEATHER!

IF I SAID I WANTED TO LEAVE, WOULD YOU DO IT...
WHITE THING?

GRR

THANK YOU...
...MOKONA!

FINE.
WHILE YOU'RE ON THIS WORLD, I'LL VOUCH FOR YOU.
SHFT

SEE...
GYU
I OWE YÛKO-SAN A FAVOR.

RLL RLL RLL
THIS IS AN APARTMENT BUILDING. WE'VE GOT ROOM.
YOU CAN USE THESE ROOMS UNTIL YOU GO TO YOUR NEXT WORLD.
THANK YOU VERY MUCH!

IT'S AFTER MIDNIGHT ALREADY.
IT'S TIME TO SLEEP.
I'LL SHOW YOU TO YOUR ROOMS.

FAI AND KUROGANE, YOU DON'T MIND SHARING, DO YOU?
NOT AT ALL!
WHAT WAS THAT?!
RATTL
RATTL

YOU CAN USE THIS ROOM.
WHY DO I HAVE TO STAY WITH A COMPLETE STRANGER!
I'M NOT A STRANGER! I TOLD YOU MY NAME, DIDN'T I?
RATTL RATTL
THANK YOU VERY MUCH.

MOKONA TOLD YOU MOKONA'S NAME!
YOU'RE STRANGER THAN ALL THE REST!
AND SAKURA-SAN . . .

I...
...WANT TO STAY BY HER SIDE.

VERY WELL.
BUT YOU MUST GET AT LEAST SOME SLEEP FOR YOURSELF.
YOU HAVE NO IDEA WHAT AWAITS YOU OR WHAT WILL HAPPEN IN THIS COUNTRY.
WHEN THERE IS A CHANCE TO SLEEP, YOU SHOULD SLEEP.

YOU'LL BE PROTECTED BY MY HONEY AND MYSELF.
ぴょん
BOING
RELAX AND SLEEP TONIGHT.
モコナ小狼と寝るー
MOKONA WILL SLEEP WITH SYAORAN!

ALL RIGHT.

パタン
KACHAK
ばいばい
BYE BYE!

WHERE...
...AM I?

SOMEONE'S COMING?!

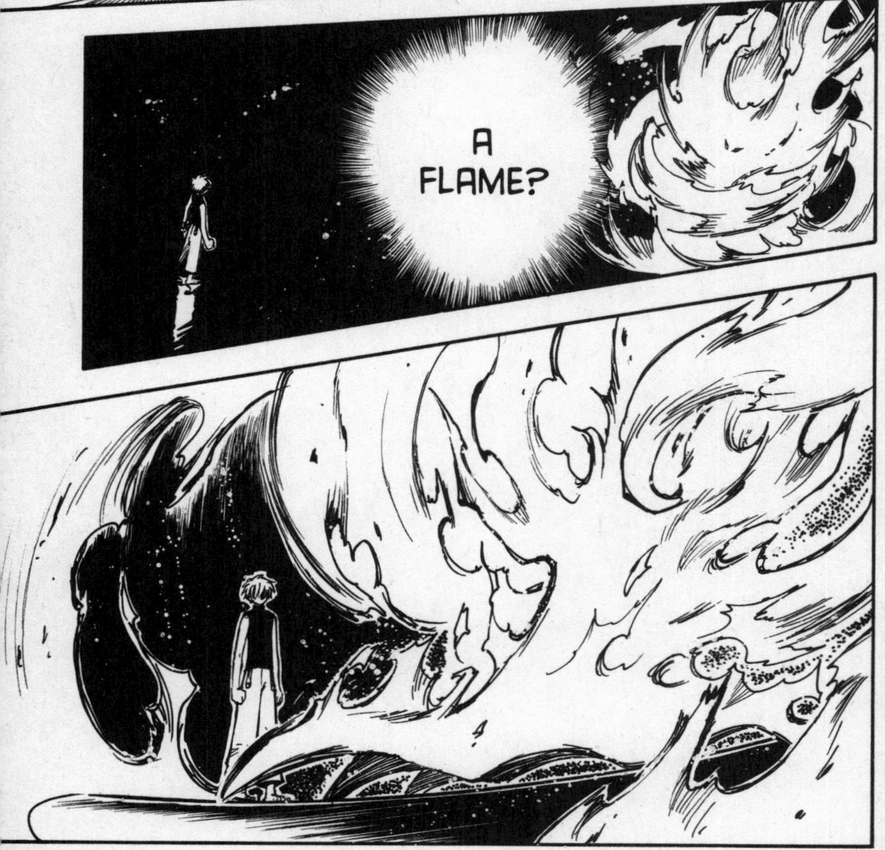
A FLAME?

I...
...AM THE MASTER OF THOSE WHO UTILIZE FLAME.
I HAVE BEEN SEARCHING FOR A SUITABLE SUBJECT FOR A VERY LONG TIME.
DO YOU WANT POWER?
I DO.

YOU MAY TAKE ME IF YOU WISH POWER...
...BUT WHAT WILL YOU DO WITH IT...
...BOY?
YOU HAVE A STRONG HEART, THINKING ONLY OF THE ONE YOU LOVE.
YOU ARE THE ONE I SEARCHED FOR.
I WILL PROTECT A PERSON PRECIOUS TO ME.

GASP
FUUU
ZZYA ZZYA
A DREAM ?
IT'S...
...WARM?

Chapitre.5
The Instant of Awakening

AND SO...
YOU GUYS WON'T GET ANYTHING DONE SITTING IN YOUR ROOMS.
YOU HAVE TO START YOUR SEARCH FOR SAKURA'S FEATHER SOMEPLACE!
SO GET OUT INTO THE NEIGHBOR-HOOD AND SEE.
HANSHIN
Republic
OKAAAY!
FINE.
.....
OH, NO!
IF THE TEACHER'S LATE, THEN THE WHOLE CLASS WILL BE CHAOS!
IT'S ABOUT TIME FOR MY LESSON TO START!
IF YOU WALK AROUND, I THINK YOU'LL BEGIN TO FIGURE OUT WHAT THIS KUDAN TALK IS ABOUT.
ALL RIGHT.

I'LL STAY BY SAKURA-SAN'S SIDE FOR YOU.
AHIRU
DUCK
THANK YOU.

IS THE WHITE THING COMING ALONG, TOO?
MOKONA ISN'T A WHITE THING! MOKONA IS MOKONA!
ばっ
BAA
STAY AWAY!

YOU HAVE TO TAKE MOKONA, OR YOU'LL PASS THE FEATHER BY AND NEVER KNOW!
DON'T WORRY. NOBODY WILL GIVE MOKONA A SECOND THOUGHT.
IF MOKONA IS A WHITE THING, THEN THIS GUY HERE IS A BLACK THING, RIGHT?
RIGHT!
あぁ～?!
GRRRR
WHAT I MEAN IS THIS WORLD IS USED TO WEIRD SIGHTS.
HUH?

CAUSE HE'S THE ONE WHO LOOKS THE MOST TRUSTWORTHY!

YUP!

GLINT

NOD

GLINT

WHAT'S *THAT* SUPPOSED TO MEAN?

AH HA HA HA HA HA

IT SURE IS A BUSTLING PLACE!
PEOPLE ALL OVER THE PLACE!
EVERY-THING'S WEIRD HERE!
SMALL BUILDINGS ARE BUNCHED UP NEXT TO THE HUGE ONES!

SYAORAN-KUN, HAVE YOU EVER SEEN THIS KIND OF THING?
HUP UP
NO. NEVER.

KURO-TAN, HOW ABOUT YOU?
TWRL
NEVER!
AND WHY DO YOU HAVE TO CALL ME BY WEIRDER AND WEIRDER NAMES?!
GRR

MOKONA HAS MANY GIRLFRIENDS!
BEH HEH!
BLUSH BLUSH
VSSH
AND ROUND!
IT'S PURE WHITE!
TEE HEE HEE
THEY AREN'T GIRLFRIENDS!!
TEE HEE
IT'S YOU THEY'RE LAUGHING AT.

COME IN, COME IN!
MOTOH GREEN GROCERY
OH ...
COME IN, GENTLE-MEN!

YOU WANNA BUY AN APPLE FROM ME?

EH?

THAT... IS AN APPLE?
IF IT ISN'T, I HAVE NO IDEA WHAT IT IS!
mo TO EEN GRO

SO IT DIDN'T LOOK LIKE THAT ON YOUR WORLD?
ZHOOP
HM?
THE SHAPE IS THE SAME, BUT IN MY WORLD, THE COLOR IS A PALE YELLOW.

ISN'T THAT CALLED A PEAR?
NO.
A PEAR IS REDDER AND HAS LEAVES COMING OUT OF THE TOP.
NO, THAT'S A RAKI SEED, ISN'T IT?

AND ...
...DO YOU WANT IT OR NOT?!
OOP!
ZUU UIP
MAKE UP YOUR MIND!
WAAA!

WANT IT!!

NICE DOIN' BUSINESS WITH YA.
HUH?

CHOMP
THESE APPLES ARE PRETTY GOOD, HUH?
YES.
WHAT IS THIS TASTE?
BUT ...
...IT REALLY IS TRUE THAT THE THREE OF US COME FROM COMPLETELY DIFFERENT CULTURES.

COME TO THINK OF IT, I NEVER ASKED... HOW DID YOU GET TO THE SHOP OF THE DIMENSION WITCH, SYAORAN-KUN?
YOU SAID THAT THERE WAS NO MAGIC IN YOUR WORLD, DIDN'T YOU?
BOING

THERE'S A HIGH PRIEST IN MY LAND. HE SENT ME.
AHHH!
THAT'S IMPRESSIVE. IT'S HARD ENOUGH TO SEND ONE PERSON ACROSS DIMENSIONS. BUT HE SENT TWO.

HOW ABOUT YOU, KURO-RIN?
GULP
I TOLD YOU TO STOP THAT!

THE PRINCESS OF MY COUNTRY SENT ME AWAY—BY FORCE.

YOU DID SOMETHING BAD AND SHE DID IT TO SCOLD YOU!
AND DON'T POINT!
AH HA HA HA
SHE DID IT TO SCOLD YOU!
YEAH! YEAH!
うるせーっての!!
WILL YOU ALL SHUT UP ?!
WHAT ABOUT YOU? WHO SENT YOU?
ME?
EHH?
ああ?!
NO ONE. I SENT MYSELF THERE.
THEN YOU DIDN'T HAVE TO ASK THE WOMAN FOR ANYTHING! YOU COULD HAVE DONE THIS YOURSELF!
何のってんだ!
WHERE DO YOU THINK YOU'RE SITTING?
えへへー
EH HEH HEH
NOT EVEN CLOSE.
WERE I TO MUSTER ALL OF MY MAGICAL ABILITIES, JUST GETTING MY-SELF FROM ONE DIMENSION TO THE NEXT WOULD TAKE EVERYTHING I CAN DO.

THE ONE WHO SENT SYAORAN-KUN...
...AND THE ONE WHO SENT YOU, KURO-CHIN...
ころん
I TOLD YOU NOT TO CALL ME NAMES!
YEAH!
...ARE PEOPLE WITH A *LOT* OF MAGIC POWER.
BUT...
...I'LL BET IT TOOK ALL THEY HAD.
I IMAGINE ANYONE HAS THE POWER TO SEND SOMEONE TO ANOTHER WORLD ONLY *ONCE*.
THAT'S THE REASON THAT YOUR HIGH PRIEST SENT YOU TO THE WITCH'S PLACE.

IT WOULD TAKE GOING TO A LOT OF WORLDS TO BE ABLE TO COLLECT ALL OF SAKURA-CHAN'S FEATHERS.
AND I THINK THE ONLY ONE WHO CAN SEND SOMEONE TO MANY WORLDS IS THE DIMENSION WITCH.
"YOUR HIGHNESS, WOULD YOU HAVE AN APPLE?"
"THANK YOU!"

UMM...
ONE OF THE TOWNSPEOPLE BROUGHT A BUNCH OF APPLES TO THE CASTLE!
UMPH
I SAVED A SHARE FOR YOU!
THE PERSON HEARD THAT I LIKED APPLES...
HERE! HAVE THEM!

EVERYONE IN THIS KINGDOM LOVES YOU, PRINCESS!
BLUSH

.....
SAKURA!
HUH?
AAAAAHHH!
WHAT'S THIS?
CLAMOR
CLAMOR
SHAKK

THIS TIME WE'RE GOING TO KICK YOUR BUTTS AND TAKE OVER THIS NEIGHBORHOOD!
ZLOOP
STMP
STMP
WHOOO!
THEY'RE COOL!
YAAAAHH!
ANOTHER ROPED-OFF BATTLE!

THAT BASTARD HAS A SPECIAL KUDAN...
HA?
...BUT DON'T LET THAT GO TO YOUR HEAD!
KUDAN?!
JEET
KLNCH
YAAAHH!
YAAAHH!
IT'S SO... HOT?!

SWIT
SHAKK

HUH?
GWAA
DOO
GM
GM
GM
GM
SO THAT'S A KUDAN?
YAA AHH!
WHAT IS WRONG WITH KIDS THESE DAYS?
YAA AHH!
YAA AHH!
YOU DARN BRATS!
I THINK I'VE FIGURED OUT WHY NO ONE WAS SURPRISED AT MOKONA.
IT'S THOSE GUYS AGAIN!

GM GM
VASSH
DO-SHAK
ZU
GRAAA
HEH!

GWAASSH

EYAAAAAHH!!
AIEEEE!
YAAAHH! YAAAHH!
ZLOOOOM
DOSHAA
AAAHH!
AAAHH!
WATCH OUT!!
GWAA

VAA AA
NO OOO

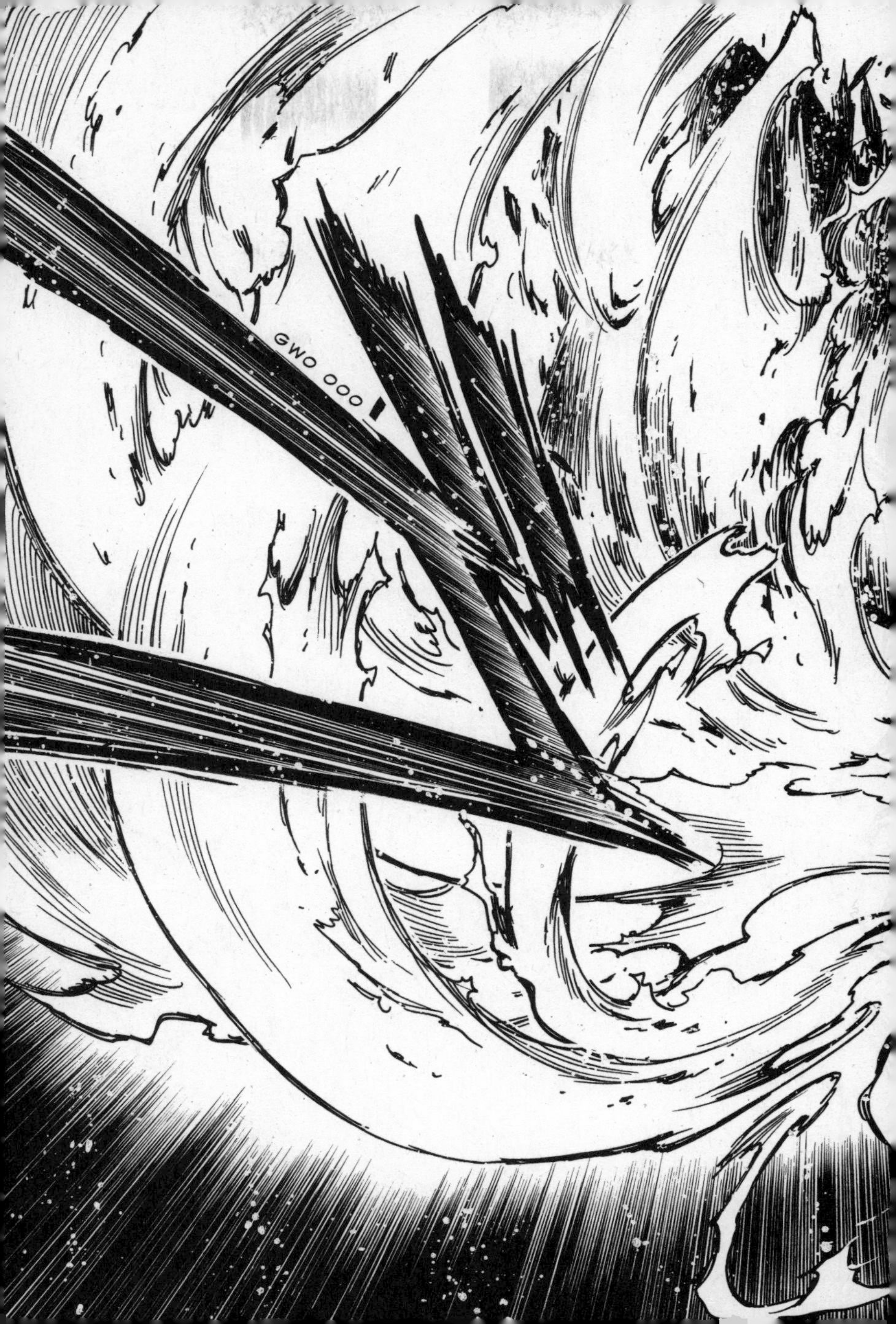
GWO OOO

GWOOOOOOOO

YOU SEEM TO HAVE A SPECIAL KUDAN, DON'T YOU?

Past Works

CLAMP have created many series. Here is a brief overview of one of them.

Cardcaptor Sakura: Master of the Clow

The first volume of *Cardcaptor Sakura* was released in Japan in 1996, and by the time the series was finished it would number twelve volumes in all. The first story arc, wherein Sakura would capture all of the Clow Cards and be named Master of the Clow, encompassed the first six volumes. In the final six volumes, Sakura discovers that there is another type of magic beyond that represented by the Clow Cards, and she must tap an inner power she didn't know she had in order to combat it. In Japan, there were twelve volumes all called *Cardcaptor Sakura*; in America, the second six have been released as *Cardcaptor Sakura: Master of the Clow*.

Romance abounds in this second arc, with Sakura still trying to manage her serious crush on Yukito, and Li Syaoran and new transfer student Eriol Hirragizawa both showing interest in Sakura. When Eriol turns out to be the reincarnation of the wizard Clow Reed, creator of the cards that bear his name, a series of magical tests begin for Sakura, whose purpose becomes apparent only later in the series.

In fact, romance is what it's all about in the closing chapter of the series. Sakura confesses her love for Yukito, only to have Yukito deny her, because he's in love with her older brother Tôya! Eriol finds his true love, Kaho, and Li Syaoran finally finds the courage to tell Sakura how he really feels.

Clearly, CLAMP felt very close to these characters and wanted to go on telling their stories—which they have done in the pages of *Tsubasa*, and, to a lesser extent, in *xxxHOLiC*!

Dramatis Personae

You'd need a scorecard to keep track of all the characters who will be appearing in *Tsubasa* and *xxxHOLiC*, so we've decided to create one for you. Some of these characters will look familiar, but you haven't really met most of them before. Don't read these if you haven't read this volume yet—there's a reason we put them at the end of the book!

Sakura

While it's clear that Sakura is older than her counterpart from *Cardcaptor Sakura*, we don't actually know her age yet. She is the princess of Clow, raised by her brother, King Tôya. She's a happy princess, well-loved by her people. Sakura possesses the power to change the world, but it will be a while before she—or we—understand what that means.

Syaoran

Syaoran's father died in an archaeological dig, leaving him an orphan, but Syaoran felt compelled to continue his father's work. He's closer than ever to uncovering the secrets of the giant wings buried in the sand, but a threat to Sakura's safety sends him on a quest to save her life! The *Tsubasa* version of Syaoran is very different from the character in *Cardcaptor Sakura*. Where the *CS* Syaoran is dour, surly, even rude at times, *Tsubasa*'s version is open, friendly—and clearly in love with Sakura.

Tomoyo

In *CS*, Tomoyo was Sakura's best friend who videotaped her card-capturing exploits. In *Tsubasa*, Tomoyo is the queen of another realm, and like Yukito, she is a powerful sorceress. It remains to be seen if her role in this drama is concluded.

Fai D. Flowright

Fai's motivation for visiting Yûko, the space-time witch, isn't entirely clear. Like Tomoyo, he is the ruler of his land of Seresu. He may be fleeing a battle he's lost, or he may desperately need to get away from a battle he's won—we just don't know yet. What we do know is that he is the creator of this world's version of Chi, a character from CLAMP's *Chobits*, and that he is fleeing from Ashura, a variation of the main character of CLAMP's first series, *RG Veda*.

Chi

In *Chobits*, Chi was a persocom, a personal computer found by Hideki Motosuwa. With her memory wiped clean, Chi and Hideki have a lot of work to do to discover her origins. Along the way, each discovers a lot more about themselves and about their feelings for each other. Of course, that's assuming that a machine can even have feelings in the first place...

The *Tsubasa* version of Chi was created by Fai, so she is clearly *not* the same character as in *Chobits*, although her personality appears remarkably similar. As Fai begins his quest, he leaves Chi behind to guard against King Ashura's awakening.

Yûko

Yûko is a witch. She lives in a peculiar house in Tokyo with two peculiar helpers, Maru and Moru. Her work is simple: She helps people . . . for a price. The price is never more than her customer can bear, but the greater the need, the higher it gets. Yûko is something of an enigma: She comes across as very mysterious and all-knowing, but she also has a playful, sometimes wild side that leads to unfortunate side effects. Like hangovers.

Watanuki

Watanuki Kimihiro will pop up in *Tsubasa* from time to time, but his home is over in *xxxHOLiC*, where he works for Yûko, cleaning, cooking, gardening, and doing whatever other chores Yûko can come up with. It's the price he pays for Yûko to grant his wish—to be rid of the spirit visions that haunt him. Although he's a hard worker, he often finds working for Yûko to be a frustrating experience.

Sorata (Sora) Arisugawa

When Sora was three years old, the Buddhist monks of Mt. Koya recognized Sora as a future Dragon of Heaven. Knowing that he would develop powers that could help to save the earth, the monks started training him, and Sora's irrepressible personality turned the monastery upside down. But when the three-year-old Sora was parted from his mother, the tears in her eyes affected him deeply. He determined that he would find the one girl for him, and he would protect her. He would protect her and die for her so that she may never feel hurt the way his mother did. In the story of X (*X/1999*), the girl he found was Arashi Kishu.

Arashi Kishu

At age six, Arashi was wandering the streets eating out of garbage cans and wondering if life was really worth it. Her mother had died three months earlier, and although she had asked Arashi to survive somehow, Arashi was beginning to have second thoughts. Being found by her mother's old Shinto teacher and brought into a beautiful shrine still didn't answer Arashi's question of whether to die or go on living. The promise of becoming a Dragon of Heaven, and more importantly, having friends in the future so that she wouldn't be alone, made Arashi decide to give life a try. In the story of X (*X/1999*), she grew into a Shinto "miko" priestess and joined the Seven Seals.

Translation Notes

Japanese is a tricky language for most westerners, and translation is often more art than science. For your edification and reading pleasure, here are notes on some of the places where we could have gone in a different direction in our translation of the work, or where a Japanese cultural reference is used.

The Kingdom of Clow

Made up of the characters Eternal and Tower, the pronunciation *kurô* sounds suspiciously like Clow.

Intimacy

After Sakura and Syaoran's conversation, you should notice a distinct similarity between that conversation and the later one of Tôya and Yukito. It's all about intimacy. Once two people are close enough friends, they drop the honorifics and titles (see *Honorifics* at the front of the book) and the grammar of polite language, and they become more direct and easygoing.

Ginryû

The characters for Ginryû mean "silver dragon," which gives you the reason for the dragon on the hilt.

Hitsuzen

This is actually defined by Yûko in *xxxHOLiC* Volume 1: "Hitsuzen. A naturally foreordained event. A state in which other outcomes are impossible. A result which can only be obtained by a single causality, and other causalities would necessarily create different results."

Kuro-chan, Kuro-rin . . .

All of the names that Fai is trying to give Kurogane are the type of nicknames that one would give cute high-school girls (ko-gals), or that cute high-school girls would give themselves.

Sora's Accent

Accents in Japanese and English work somewhat differently. In English, an accent is mostly marked by pronunciation—especially of the vowel sounds—and a few differences in vocabulary. So if you take a little time to get used to the differences, you will have no problem understanding even the thickest accent in English. In Japanese, there are some pronunciation differences, but most of the differences are in vocabulary. Since the differences start at the core vocabulary (even the ubiquitous verb "to be"!), and spread throughout, a thick accent is nearly as difficult to understand as a completely different language. Fortunately for most Japanese citizens, the Osaka dialect is very popular in the media, so everyone is used to the different words, even if they didn't grow up in the Osaka area.

The logo for the Hanshin Tigers

The Hanshin Republic

For those who don't know Japanese baseball, the most popular team in Japan is the Yomiuri Giants. The second most popular team is the Hanshin Tigers, and like other second-mosts, the fans of the Hanshin Tigers are fiercely competitive and fanatical. None more than Sora's character, and so, the Hanshin Republic is the fondest dream of Tigers' fans—an entire nation devoted body and soul to Osaka's favorite baseball club. More on this in Volume 2!

Tsubasa Volume 2 Contents

ツバサ
RESERVoir CHRoNiCLE

Chapitre.6
Strength of the Heart

GWOO
OOOOO

A KUDAN THAT CAN WIELD FIRE...
MINE WORKS WATER AND YOURS, FIRE.
THIS WILL BE INTEREST-ING!

GYAAAAH
ZYOOOOO
KA PAAH
DOOH

I'M SHÔGO ASAGI.
YOU?
..... SYAORAN.
SSSHHHH

I LIKE YOUR STYLE.
SSSHHHHH

SHÔGO, THE COPS!
YA-AHH!

AND IT WAS JUST GETTING GOOD.
SIGH

COME ON, YA BASTARDS!
LET'S GET OUTTA HERE!
FOWOOO!!
HOOOSH
HOOSH
HOOSH
HOOSH
HOOSH
NEXT TIME WE MEET, WE'LL HAVE SOME REAL FUN!
THMP
TMP TMP
HOLD IT!!
TMP

!?
FWOOM
GHOOOOO
SHULOOM
IT... WENT... INSIDE ME.

THAT WAS AMAZING! SYAORAN-KUN, DID THAT COME FROM YOU?

THAT'S A "KUDAN," HUH?
I'M NOT SURE. BUT I SUDDENLY GOT VERY HOT...

あ! OH!
YOU'RE OKAY, RIGHT?
NOD NOD
AND YOU, YOU'RE OKAY, TOO?
I'M GLAD FOR THAT!
BOW
HOOSH
EHH?!
HE VANISHED!
OH!
PAPH
THAT KID WAS A KUDAN!
THESE KUDAN...
IT LOOKS LIKE THEY CAN BE ANY-THING!

NOW, WHERE CAN MY "ALMOST KUDAN" HAVE GOTTEN OFF TO?
HMM?
GLANCE
GASP
MOKONA!!

AAAH!
IT PROBABLY GOT STEPPED ON SOMEWHERE AROUND HERE.
LIKE SOME DISCARDED PORK BUN.
WHAT A PAIN!
めんどくせー
ぽりぽり
SKRITCH SKRITCH
いやー
NOOOO.
ほら
LOOK..
THE TRUTH IS QUITE DIFFERENT.

IT'S SO CUTE!
KYAA!
きゃ
KYAA!
きゃ
KYAA!
きゃ
THE SWEETEST THING!
LOOK HOW SOFT!
MOKONA IS POPULAR WITH THE LADIES!

BYE-BYE!
バイバーイ
キャー
KYAA!
キャー
KYAA!
BYE-BYE!
バイバーイ
MOKONA, WHERE WERE YOU?
ON TOP OF KUROGANE.
BUT THEN, MOKONA FELL OFF!
BUT JUST EARLIER...
... MOKONA WENT...
LISTEN!
聞ーて!
LISTEN!
聞ーて!
めきょ
BOINK
... JUST LIKE THIS!!
BUT NOBODY PAID ANY ATTENTION!
YOU MEAN THAT SAKURA'S FEATHER IS SOMEWHERE NEARBY?

IT WAS ...
BUT MOKONA DOESN'T FEEL IT ANYMORE.
DID YOU FIGURE OUT WHO HAD IT?
DON'T KNOW.
ふるる
SHAKE SHAKE
SHAKE
OH ...
I SEE.
しょんぼり
GLOOM

うーん
HMM.
EVEN IF WE LIMIT IT TO THE PEOPLE WHO WERE HERE, IT'LL STILL BE A LONG SEARCH.
THERE WERE LOTS OF PEOPLE.
STILL, WE NOW KNOW THAT SOMEONE CLOSE BY HAS IT.
THAT'S PRETTY GOOD PROG-RESS.
AND IF YOU SENSE ANYTHING MORE, LET US KNOW.
THUMP
YES!
MOKONA WILL GO ALL-OUT!

BUT IF KURO-CHI NEVER DROPPED MOKONA, THIS WOULDN'T HAVE HAPPENED.
WHAT MAKES THIS MY FAULT! AND WILL YOU STOP CALLING ME THOSE NAMES?!
BOW
I JUST WANTED TO THANK YOU!
MY NAME IS MASAYOSHI SAITÔ.
PLEASE LET ME DO SOMETHING FOR YOU IN THANKS!
NO, WE REALLY DIDN'T DO ANYTHING . . .
BUT . . . BUT . . .
MOKONA WANTS LUNCH!!
SOMETHING REALLY GOOD!
はーい
HEEEERE!
GUIDE US THERE.
教えて!
EH?
OKAY!
はいっ

32番街

営業中

SSSZZZZ

WHAT IS...
STARE
B-BMP
B-BMP

あの あの
UMM... UMM...
Y'SEE... OKONOMIYAKI IS *MY* FAVORITE DISH, SO...
I ORDERED MODAN-YAKI, BUT MAYBE TONPEI-YAKI WOULD HAVE BEEN BETTER.
"OKONO-MIYAKI"? IS THAT WHAT THIS IS CALLED?

えっ?
EH?
OKONO-MIYAKI IS A STAPLE OF THE DIET IN THE HANSHIN REPUBLIC.
IF YOU DON'T KNOW, THEN THAT MUST MEAN...

AH!
...YOU COME FROM OUTSIDE THE COUNTRY?
STARE
YOU'VE GOT BLOND HAIR, TOO.
"OUTSIDE"? YOU COULD SAY THAT.
??
DO THOSE PEOPLE ALWAYS RUN ROUGHSHOD AROUND THIS DISTRICT?
THE GUYS WITH THE CAPS AND THE ONES IN THE GOGGLES?
THAT WAS...
...A FIGHT FOR DOMINANCE.
THEY FORM INTO TEAMS AND FIGHT TO SEE WHOSE KUDAN IS THE STRONGER.
AND ...
...THE STRONGEST CLAIMS THE RIGHTS TO THE TERRITORY?

BUT THINK OF THE LIVES PUT IN DANGER WHEN THEY FIGHT IN SUCH A LARGE PUBLIC PLACE.
THIS OKONOMIYAKI LOOKS GREAT!
THAT'S BECAUSE I'M JUST USELESS.
STARE
THAT'S TRUE, HUH?
MASAYOSHI-KUN HERE WAS IN BIG TROUBLE.

THERE . . .
. . . THERE ARE BAD TEAMS, BUT THERE ARE GOOD TEAMS, TOO!

THEY PATROL THEIR TERRITORY MAKING SURE NO BAD KIDS CAUSE TROUBLE.
AND IF BAD PEOPLE ARE AROUND, THEY TAKE CARE OF THE PROBLEM!

LIKE A LOCAL MILITIA?
WHAT ABOUT THOSE TWO TEAMS BEFORE?

THE ONES IN CAPS WERE THE BAD ONES!
BUT THE ONES IN GOGGLES AREN'T LIKE THEM AT ALL!
WHEN THEY BATTLE OTHER TEAMS, SOME OF THE SURROUNDING BUILDINGS GET DAMAGED, SO THE ADULTS ARE AFRAID OF THEM . . . BUT THEY WOULDN'T DO ANYTHING ELSE THAT'S BAD!
THEY'RE REALLY COOL!

ESPECIALLY THEIR LEADER, SHÔGO-SAN!
THEY SAY HIS KUDAN IS SPECIAL LEVEL!
IT'S SO BIG AND STRONG... EVERYONE WISHES THEY HAD A KUDAN JUST LIKE IT!
OH!
SMELLS GREAT!
STARE
ZLIP ZLIP
S-LUMP
BLUSH
STARE
I... I'M SORRY.
I-I SURE DO!
LOOK AT ALL THE CABBAGE!

THUMPA
THUMPA
THUMPA
AND YOU WISH YOU HAD A FRIEND JUST LIKE HIM, HUH?
STARE
STAAAAARE

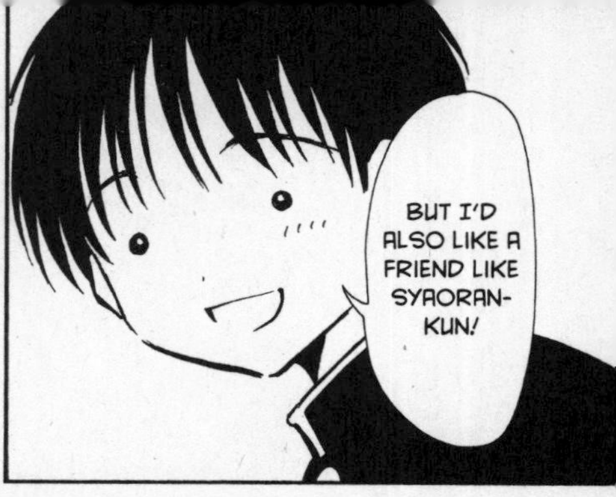
BUT I'D ALSO LIKE A FRIEND LIKE SYAORAN-KUN!

EH?

ANYBODY WITH A SPECIAL-LEVEL KUDAN ...
... IS JUST AMAZING!
鶴橋 風月

STARE
DIDN'T THE LEADER OF THAT GOGGLE TEAM SAY SOMETHING ABOUT A SPECIAL KUDAN ...?
HMM.
SO, WHAT IS THAT?
SPECIAL LEVEL?

IT'S AN ESPECIALLY HIGH LEVEL FOR A KUDAN.

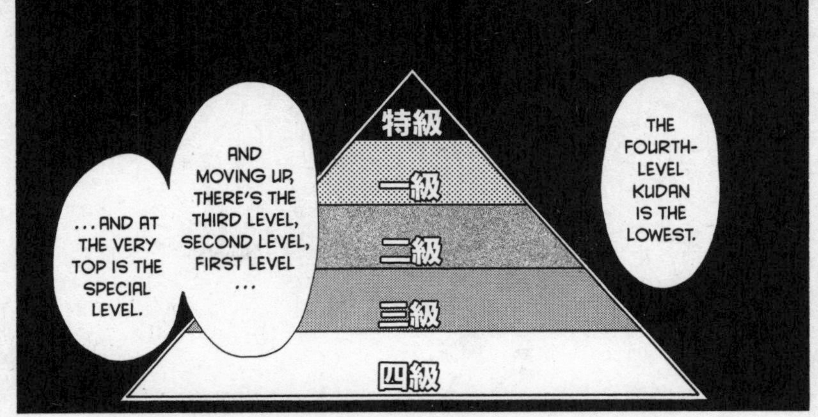
THE FOURTH-LEVEL KUDAN IS THE LOWEST.
AND MOVING UP, THERE'S THE THIRD LEVEL, SECOND LEVEL, FIRST LEVEL ...
...AND AT THE VERY TOP IS THE SPECIAL LEVEL.
特級
一級
二級
三級
四級

YEARS AGO, ALL THE COUNTRIES GOT TOGETHER AND BANNED THE USE OF LEVELS ON KUDAN...
...BUT NORMAL PEOPLE STILL USE THE SYSTEM.
TWTCH
THEN ...
...THAT LEADER'S KUDAN MUST BE VERY STRONG.
YEAH!

SO IS SYAORAN-KUN'S!
TO GET A STRONG KUDAN, ESPECIALLY A SPECIAL-LEVEL KUDAN, YOU NEED TO BE A STRONG PERSON YOUR-SELF, OR THEY WON'T STAY!
IT'S A PERSON'S HEART THAT CONTROLS A KUDAN.
SO IF A PERSON CAN COMMAND A STRONG KUDAN, THAT'S PROOF THAT THE PERSON IS STRONG!
WHO WOULDN'T WANT A FRIEND LIKE THAT?
MY KUDAN ...
... IS FOURTH LEVEL— THE VERY BOTTOM.
KLNCH
MASAYOSHI-KUN ...

BUT *WHEN* DID SYAORAN-KUN'S KUDAN JOIN UP WITH HIM?
TWTCH
TWTCH
TWTCH
HMM?
NOW THAT YOU MEN-TION IT . . .

SWIPP
HM?
夢?
A DREAM?
I HAD AN ODD DREAM LAST NIGHT.

STOP RIGHT THERE !!
SWATT
POIT
EYAAH!
GMM

DOOOM
YOUR MAJESTY!
AND THE HIGH PRIEST!

Chapitre.7
Linked Worlds

ツバサ
RESERVoir CHRoNiCLE

Y— YOUR MAJESTY, WHAT BRINGS YOU HERE?
EHP?
EHP?
HENH?
YOU GOT THE WRONG GUY.
"YOUR MAJESTY" IS NOWHERE IN MY NAME.
WHAT?
AND MISTER ...
...WE DO THE FLIPPING HERE.
IF YOU'D JUST LEAVE IT AND WAIT, WE'LL BE RIGHT THERE.
Y— YES, SIR!

"YOUR MAJESTY"! THAT SOUNDS COOL!
LEAVE IT, WILL YA?

MAJESTY... WAS HE A KING IN YOUR WORLD?
YES...

AND THE GUY WITH HIM WAS THE HIGH PRIEST...
IS THAT RIGHT...?
WITH OKONOMIYAKI HERE, THE WAITERS DO ALL THE COOKING FOR YOU.
YOU DON'T HAVE TO DO ANYTHING.
BUSTLE
てきぱき

うるせー
SHADDUP!
IT'S JUST LIKE THE SPACE-TIME WITCH SAID...
しかられた
YOU GOT YELLED AT!

"PEOPLE YOU'VE MET ON YOUR WORLD..."
"...THEY'VE DEVELOPED UNDER COMPLETELY DIF-FERENT CONDITIONS ON OTHER WORLDS."

THEY'RE THE SAME... AND NOT THE SAME.
EXCUSE ME?
THE TWO FROM SYAORAN'S WORLD LIVED A COMPLETELY DIFFERENT LIFE THAN THESE TWO.

YOU'RE SAYING THAT THEY'RE THE SAME AS THE KING AND HIGH PRIEST OF THE KID'S WORLD?

BUT WHEN IT COMES DOWN TO IT...
...AT THE VERY BASIC LEVEL, THEY'RE THE SAME.
I GUESS.

BASIC LEVEL?
THE VERY ROOT OF THEIR LIVES.
THEIR NATURE... THEIR HEARTS...
"SOUL"!
THAT'S WHAT YOU'RE SAYING, RIGHT?

FROM NOW ON, I'M CALLING YOU, "YOUR MAJESTY."
DON'T YOU DARE!
I WONDER IF HIS MAJESTY AND THE HIGH PRIEST ARE ALL RIGHT.
DID THE COUNTRY CARRY ON ALL RIGHT AFTER THE FIGHT?
YES.
THOSE TWO WOULD MAKE SURE EVERY-THING'S FINE.

AND I MUST DO EVERYTHING POSSIBLE . . .
. . . TO SAVE THE LIFE OF THE PRINCESS!
. . . TO RETURN THE FEATHERS OF SAKURA'S MEMORY!

SYAORAN-KUN?
HUH?
IF YOU DON'T EAT IT, WE WILL.
THESE "CHOPSTICKS" ARE HARD TO USE!
OKAY!
AH! あの…
WE CAN ORDER ANOTHER!
DOWN THE HATCH!
いっただきまーす!
LISTEN YOU!
THIS ONE'S MINE!!
GRATCH
TUGG TUGG TUGG

THAT WAS...
...GREAT!!
MMPAAAAAHH

IT REALLY WAS.
GOOD JOB GUIDING US HERE.
IT REALLY DID TASTE GOOD!
OPEN

GLARE
IF YOU KNOW ANY OTHER GOOD PLACES, TELL US!
"TAKO-YAKI," FRIED OCTOPUS, IS REALLY GOOD, TOO!

NOW...
WHAT'S THE PLAN FROM HERE?
I THOUGHT WE WOULD SEARCH IN THIS SECTION OF TOWN.

HM.
BUT WE DON'T KNOW OUR WAY AROUND, SO WE WON'T BE ABLE TO GO FAR.
WE HAVE TO BE ABLE TO FIND OUR WAY BACK TO SORA CHAN'S APARTMENT.
UH... EXCUSE ME.

ARE YOU GUYS GOING SOME-WHERE?
YES.
WHERE WOULD THAT BE?
WE DON'T REALLY KNOW. WE'RE SEARCH-ING FOR SOME-THING.

IF IT'S OKAY WITH YOU, I'LL HELP YOU LOOK.
I CAN SHOW YOU AROUND.
WE DON'T WANT TO PUT YOU OUT...
NOT AT ALL!
BUT I SHOULD PHONE HOME FIRST.
IF YOU'D JUST WAIT HERE A SECOND...
TMP

MOKONA WILL MAKE A PHONE CALL, TOO!
HELLO? HELLO? HELLO?
TMP TMP
TMP
HE REALLY DOES WANT TO BE FRIENDS, HUH?

STARE

I NEARLY FORGOT.
OUR CONVERSATION WAS CUT OFF.
YOU WERE TALKING ABOUT YOUR DREAM ...
YES ...
IT WAS ABOUT THAT CREATURE THAT APPEARED ...
...THAT BEAST OF FIRE.

IF YOU'RE TALKING ABOUT DREAMS OF WEIRD ANIMALS ... I HAD ONE, TOO.
ME, AS WELL.
IT WAS VERY PERSISTENT.
STAMP
I WANNA KNOW WHO THIS "SYAORAN" IS.

YOU HAVE BUSINESS WITH HIM?
ARE YOU THE ONE WHO SHÔGO SAID HE "LIKES YOUR STYLE"?
DOOM
へにゃっ
HEH HENH
AND WHAT IF I AM?
......

I'M SYAORAN.
A LITTLE KID?
ARE YOU SERIOUS?
NO, HE'S THE GUY! I'M SURE OF IT!
AND YOUR PLAN IS TO JOIN SHÔGO'S TEAM?
TEAM?
SHÔGO ALREADY HAS TOO MANY TOP-LEVEL PEOPLE ON HIS TEAM!
ANY MORE WILL TIP THE BALANCE!
EVEN SHÔGO ADMITTED THAT YOU HAVE A REALLY STRONG KUDAN!

IF YOU INTEND TO JOIN SHÔGO'S TEAM, I'M GONNA HAVE TO STOP YOU!
ZWIP
I'M NOT JOINING.
I'M NOT JOINING YOU, EITHER.
NOT A CHANCE!
LOOKIN' GOOD, SYAORAN!
HE DOESN'T MINCE WORDS, DOES HE?
THEN YOU'LL JOIN MY TEAM!
YEAH!
YEAH!
YEAH!
YEAH!
I HAVE MY OWN AFFAIRS.
SO...
GRR
GRR
GRR
GRR
GRR
GRR
GRR
THEN YOU'RE PLANNING TO START A TEAM OF YOUR OWN!!
GRRAAAHH!
WHA-?
NO, YOU'RE NOT GET-TING—
FWAA

WELL, I'M GONNA TAKE YOU OUT RIGHT NOW!!
THAT'S HUGE!

I'M NOT DOING ANY SUCH THING!
DWOOOM
GWOOOM
BAM

ZEEEEEEEN
SSST
HMP
HMP
NOT A GOOD LISTENER, IS HE?
YAAAH!
YAAAH!
TMP TMP
YAAAH!
YAAAH!
TMP
TMP
YAAAH!
I'VE BEEN PRETTY BORED HERE.
TUMP
KRAKL

DOOM
I'LL TAKE YOU ON!

KURO-GANE'S BEEN LOOKING FORWARD TO THIS!
HE WASN'T BORED AT ALL!
THE HANSHIN REPUBLIC IS JUST HIS STYLE, HUH?
SHUT UP, OVER THERE!
ZAPH
BUT ...
...KUROGANE-SAN!
YOU GAVE YOUR SWORD TO THAT WOMAN...

THAT SWORD WAS MAGIC.
IT WAS SPECIAL.
BUT KUDAN ...
...AREN'T MONSTERS.
AND IN *MY* JAPAN, I NEEDED IT TO KILL THE MONSTERS THAT LIVED THERE.
SO... WHAT LEVEL IS *YOUR* KUDAN?
HEH
I DON'T KNOW, AND I DON'T CARE.
WHAT'S ALL THE *TALK* FOR?
COME AND GET ME!

SYAORAN-KUN!!
YAAAHH
YAAAHH
YAAAHH
MASAYOSHI-KUN, DO YOU KNOW THIS GUY?
IT'S A TEAM THAT WANTS TO CONTROL THIS DISTRICT!
THEY'RE BATTLING SHÔGO'S TEAM OVER IT!
IS THEIR LEADER ANY GOOD?

HIS KUDAN IS *FIRST LEVEL!*
HE MAY NOT LOOK LIKE MUCH, BUT HIS KUDAN IS ONE OF THE FASTEST AROUND!
AND...
TAKE A LOOK AT THE ATTACK OF A FIRST-LEVEL KUDAN!
EAT THIS!!

VWAAAM
KANI-
NABE
SENKAI!*
POK
*CRAB-POT REVOLUTION
PAKOW
ZUU
SKRRRRT
IT SLICED
RIGHT
THROUGH!
THAT KUDAN
CAN SHARPEN PARTS
OF ITS BODY TO
AN EDGE AS SHARP
AS A KNIFE!

POK
VWAAAAAMM
GO!!
GO!!
TMP
TMP
TMP
TMP
TMP
SLA KOW
WATCH OUT!!
I THINK IF YOU TRY TO GET INVOLVED, HE'LL GET REALLY MAD.
KURO-TAN'S LIKE THAT.

JAA KIIIIN
KANI DÔRAKU !!*
*CRAB FREE-STYLE
KUROGANE-SAN!!
WHERE'S YOUR KUDAN?
YOU'RE PROBABLY SO WEAK, YOU'RE ASHAMED TO BRING IT OUT!
AHHHHH
HA HA
HA HA
KRMBLE KRMBLE

OH, SHUT *UP!*
KRMBL
YOU GUYS *TALK* TOO MUCH!
MY KUDAN HAS AN EVEN TOUGHER SHELL THAN MOST FIRST-LEVEL KUDAN!
NICE, BOSS-MAN!
BUT IT HAS A WEAK-NESS.
AWW...
IF I HAD A SWORD, IT'D BE IN PIECES ALREADY.

SHWAAA
!!

SHWAAA
WHAT?!
YOU WERE THE ONE THAT APPEARED IN MY DREAM!

SHWAAAA AAA
YOU'RE ASKING ME TO WIELD YOU?
SHINGG
I GET IT.
YOU LIKE A GOOD PUNCH-UP, TOO!

ZIIING
S-SO THAT'S YOUR KUDAN? IT'S PROBABLY ALL SHOW!
WELL, I'VE GOT AN ULTIMATE ATTACK!
KANE KUI-HÔDAI !!*
VWO OOM
IT DOESN'T MATTER HOW HARD A SHELL IS, WHEN YOU PULL OUT A KNIFE ...
...LOBSTERS AND CRABS ALL HAVE WEAK POINTS IN THE JOINTS.
*ALL-YOU-CAN-EAT CRAB

HAMA RYÛ-Ô-JIN !!*
*MAGIC-WAVE DRAGON-KING SWORD

DOOOOM

GAAAAAAAAAAAAAAA!!

ARE YOU OKAY, BOSS?
HANG IN THERE!
MY KUDAN! MY KUDAAAAAN!!
YAAAH!!
YAAAH!!
YAAAH!!
YAAAH!!

TH-THE KID LIED!
HE *DID* FORM A TEAM!
YOU'RE A PART OF SYAORAN'S TEAM, AREN'T YOU?
WHEEZE
WHEEZE
I'M NOT ON *ANY*-*BODY'S* TEAM!
LISTEN ...
...IN MY LIFE, I'VE ONLY SERVED UNDER ONE PERSON!

AND THAT'S PRINCESS TOMOYO!

Chapitre.8
The Country Where Gods Live

WE'RE BACK!
KACHAK

SST
WE'RE BACK!
WE'RE BACK!
WELCOME.
COME ON IN.

WERE YOU ABLE TO FIND ANY CLUES?
TMP TMP TMP
YES!

OH!
YOU'RE ALL HERE!
HOW'D IT GO?

BUT . . .
. . . BEFORE ANY OF THAT . . .

HONEY !!
MMMMMM!
WHERE'S MY "WELCOME HOME" KISS?! ♡

PUT IT HERE, BABE!

I SEE . . .
YOU *HAD* A REACTION, BUT IT DISAPPEARED.

AND...
THROB
じん
じん
THROB
...JUST WHEN SYAORAN WAS IN TROUBLE, SOMETHING THAT LOOKED LIKE A BEAST OF FIRE SUDDENLY APPEARED.
WHAT A HUGE BUMP!
ARASHI'S REALLY STRONG
AHIRU

THAT'S RIGHT.
THAT BEAST MUST HAVE BEEN YOUR KUDAN, SYAORAN-KUN.
BOING
ぴょん

WELL...
IT SEEMS LIKE A PRETTY STRONG ONE, TOO!
AND KUROGANE'S KUDAN ALSO SEEMS STRONG!
HOW DO YOU KNOW THAT?

I TOLD YOU BEFORE . . .
. . . I'M A SCHOLAR OF HISTORY.
THE KUDAN ARE THE LINCHPIN OF THE WHOLE THING.

IT'S MY BELIEF . . .
. . . THAT KUDAN ARE AKIN TO GODS IN THIS NATION.

HANSIN
IN THE HANSHIN REPUBLIC, THERE IS A MYTH THAT'S BEEN HANDED DOWN THROUGH THE AGES . . .
...IT SAYS THAT THE NUMBER OF KAMI, GODS, IS "YAOYOROZU."

八百万
"YAOYOROZU"?
IT'S SPELLED WITH THE CHARACTERS FOR "EIGHT MILLION."

SO THERE ARE EIGHT MILLION GODS HERE?
LOTS OF...
...KAMI-SAMA!
NO, PROBABLY MANY MORE.
THEY SAY THERE ARE AS MANY GODS AS THERE ARE THINGS AND PHENOMENA IN THE WORLD.
THE WORD "YAOYOROZU" REALLY SIMPLY MEANS, "A WHOLE LOT."

SO THE GODS OF THAT MYTH ARE NOW CALLED KUDAN?
THAT'S PRETTY IMPRESSIVE.
YOU LIVE TOGETHER WITH YOUR GODS.
SO THE GODS OF THIS LAND ...
...PROTECT EACH AND EVERY PERSON WHO LIVES IN IT!
WHOOSH
YOU CAME TO THAT CONCLUSION, TOO?

I'VE THOUGHT THAT ALL ALONG!
THE KUDAN, OR RATHER THE GODS, HAVE A LASTING LOVE FOR THE PEOPLE OF THIS COUNTRY!

EVERY PERSON, WITHOUT EXCEPTION, IS ACCOM-PANIED BY A KUDAN.
SO EVERY HUMAN IN THIS COUNTRY IS PROTECTED!
NOT ONE IS LEFT ALONE!
IT'S TRUE . . .
. . . THAT A LOT OF PEOPLE IN THE HANSHIN REPUBLIC ARE EASY TO GET RILED UP.
THEY HATE LOSING; THEY NEVER GET TO THE POINT; THEY'LL ATTACK IF YOU'RE NOT PAYING ATTENTION; IF OUR TEAM WINS THEY GO CRAZY; THEY THROW THEMSELVES IN THE RIVER . . .
BUT EVEN SO . . .
. . . I THINK THEY REALLY ARE GOOD PEOPLE.

AND THAT'S WHY . . .
. . . WHEN IT COMES TO FINDING SAKURA'S FEATHER . . .
. . . SEARCHING HERE IS PROBABLY BETTER THAN SEARCHING IN A COUNTRY FULL OF BAD PEOPLE, OR A COUNTRY THAT MAKES WAR ON ITS NEIGHBORS.

.....
YES.

YOU SAID THAT YOU DETECTED THE WAVES OF SAKURA'S FEATHER, BUT YOU DON'T KNOW WHERE IT WENT?
しょぼん
SLUMP
UH-HUH.
SO IF IT WERE SIMPLY SOMEONE WHO HAD THE FEATHER AND WALKED AWAY...
...YOU PROBABLY COULD HAVE EASILY TRACKED DOWN WHERE IT WENT TO.
BUT IF THE ONE THAT HAD IT COULD APPEAR AND DISAPPEAR...
...THE ONLY THING THAT COULD HAVE IT IS...
AHIRU

GASP
A KUDAN!
IS THAT WHAT YOU MEAN?
なるほど
MAKES SENSE.
A KUDAN *CAN* APPEAR AND DISAPPEAR.
AND IF A KUDAN DISAPPEARED, THE WAVE MIGHT DIS-APPEAR, TOO.
WITHIN ONE OF THESE KUDAN...
...WE MAY FIND SAKURA'S FEATHER!
BUT WE HAVE NO IDEA JUST WHO HAD THE KUDAN WITH THE FEATHER.
IT WAS IN THE MIDDLE OF A TERRITORIAL BATTLE.
THERE WERE WHOLE LOTS OF KUDAN BACK THERE!

BUT...
...IT WOULD HAVE TO BE A STRONG KUDAN.
WHY DO YOU SAY THAT?
THE FRAGMENTS OF SAKURA'S MEMORY...
...ARE IMMENSELY POTENT—LIKE CRYSTALLIZED SHARDS OF HER HEART.
A KUDAN USES THE OWNER'S HEART.
THE STRONGER THE HEART, THE STRONGER THE KUDAN BECOMES.
IN ANY CASE...
...LOOKING FOR THE STRONGEST KUDAN SEEMS LIKE A SHORTCUT TO FINDING SAKURA'S FEATHER.
NOD
MOKONA WILL SEARCH REAL HARD!

よし!
ALL RIGHT!
SINCE WE'VE GOT THAT ALL DECIDED, IT'S TIME TO FORTIFY OURSELVES WITH SOME GOOD FOOD!
TODAY WE HAVE BEEF UDON NOODLES AND FRIED TOFU SUSHI.
I MADE ALL THE ARRANGE-MENTS BEFORE GOING OFF TO WORK.
FSSH
FSSH
I WILL NEED THE HELP OF KUROGANE AND FAI.

WHY DO I HAVE TO HELP?
IF YOU DON'T WORK, YOU DON'T EAT.
MOKONA'S GOING TO EAT, SO MOKONA WILL WORK!
I'LL HELP TOO.

NOT TODAY, YOU DON'T.
YOU WERE AWAY FROM SAKURA ALL DAY.
YOU WERE WORRIED, WEREN'T YOU?

KREEE
YOU CAN STAY AND WATCH HER.
WHEN DINNER IS READY, I'LL GIVE YOU A CALL.

THANKS!
THANKS A LOT!
KACHAK

YOUR HIGHNESS, ARE YOU ALL RIGHT?
I *TOLD* YOU TO QUIT THE "POLITE" TALK!
HMPH!
HMPH!
PLEASE FORGIVE ME—
NO... I MEAN...
SORRY.
BUT, REALLY, ARE YOU OKAY?
EH
HEH
HEH
I'M FINE.
IT'S JUST A LITTLE FEVER.
EVEN THE DOCTOR SAID THAT IT'LL GO DOWN WITH JUST A BIT OF REST.
OH!
BUT WAIT...

THEY ALSO SAY THAT IF SOMEONE HOLDS YOUR HAND ...
...YOU GET BETTER FASTER.
TOO MUCH TO ASK?
GRP
UMM...
YOU REALLY SHOULD GET SOME SLEEP.
YOU'LL STAY HERE WITH ME?
YEAH.

IF I FALL ASLEEP LIKE THIS...
...THE FIRST THING I'LL SEE WHEN I WAKE UP...
...WILL BE YOU, SYAORAN.

I'LL DO ANYTHING TO WAKE SAKURA AS QUICKLY AS I CAN!
I'LL FIND HER FEATHERS!
I WILL!

I GUESS THAT NOBODY HAS THEIR KUDAN OUT WHILE SIMPLY WALKING.
AND IF THEY DON'T, WE'LL NEVER SEE IF ANYONE'S KUDAN IS STRONGER OR WEAKER.
HANS
ラーメン
EVEN IF...
EVEN IF...
...WE DO FIND OUT WHICH KUDAN HAS TAKEN THE FEATHER...
...I DOUBT THEY'LL BE OVERLY WILLING TO GIVE IT UP.
AAH !!
GWAAAM
ぺこり
BOW

TMP
TMP
TMP
TMP
SYAORAN-KUN!!
MASA-YOSHI-KUN.
HUFF
HUFF
WHEEZE
WHEEZE
WHOOSH
WERE YOU ABLE TO FIND WHAT YOU WERE LOOKING FOR AFTER I LEFT?
NOT YET...

OKAY, THEN HOW ABOUT I BE YOUR GUIDE AGAIN TODAY?
ARE YOU SURE IT'S OKAY?
BOING
SURE!
TODAY'S SUNDAY!
IT'S PERFECTLY FINE FOR TODAY!

I'M SURPRISED YOU WERE ABLE TO FIND US.
MY KUDAN CAN FIND ANYBODY AS LONG AS HE'S MET THEM ONCE.
IT'S NO GOOD IF IT'S TOO FAR AWAY, THOUGH.

THAT'S PRETTY AMAZING!
AMAZING!
AMAZING!
BUT THAT'S ABOUT *ALL* HE CAN DO.
HE'S PRETTY WEAK!

JEEEEEEEEEN
!

GWOOON
KYAAH!
AAAAAH!!

JEEEEEN
FLIP
MOKONA!
MASAYOSHI-KUN!!
GASP
阪神城で待つ
I'll be waiting at Hanshin Castle!
DO
OOM

Chapitre.9
The Magician's Kudan

WHOOSH
FAI-
SAN!
KUROGANE-
SAN!
LOOK
AT
THIS!
!?
THIS PAPER
CAME DOWN
FROM THAT
BIRD!
阪神城で待つ
I'll be
waiting at
Hanshin
Castle!
THEY COULD
HAVE TAKEN
MOKONA AND
MASAYOSHI-
KUN TO THIS
CASTLE!

CHATTER
CHATTER
CHATTER
CHATTER
CHATTER
今◎△×鳥■◎何
飛◆◎連××？
КЦФ!!ЖЭф$Ы
Ю□Чю́Э́ЪП<У
HUH?

DONK DONK
とんとん
ЩЬКФб!?
#щЪ@ЛЖ

SKWEEK
ほじ
SKWEEK
阪神城■◎
行××▲!?

NO, IT'S NOT THAT MY EARS HAVE GONE STRANGE.
Д8Чю
SWEAT
あわ
SWEAT
あわ
違◎!
BUT FOR SOME REASON, I DON'T UNDER-STAND THE WORDS!

AND IT'S NOT AS IF WE WENT ANYWHERE!
?

AAAH!!

MOKONA!!
MEE EEE!

ぷらーん
BURUUUUM
きゃっ きゃっ
KYAA! KYAA!
うわーん
WAAAAAH!!
UMM ... ARE YOU *SURE* THIS KID IS THE ONE?
THIS IS THE GUY SHÔGO SAID HE LIKED?
ABSOLUTELY CERTAIN, MA'AM!
HE WAS WITH THE SPIKY-HAIRED BIG GUY AND THE THIN BLOND GUY.
AND ...
... THE SMALLEST ONE IN THE GROUP IS "SYAORAN."
うす!!
ZOOOM
WE HAVE A WINNER!
HMMMM.

HANSHIN CASTLE IS THIS WAY!
SUBWAY
HANSHIN CASTLE FRONT ENTRANCE STATION
HANS
CAST
TMP
TMP
TMP
TMP
ЖЪФЛ
ぼりぼり
SKRICH SKRICH
面倒◎▲!
HANSHIN MAP
I *KNEW* THEY WOULDN'T UNDER-STAND ME!

ENTR CE TO HANSH CASTLE
WHOOM

ぷらーん
BULUUUUN
MOKONA!
MASAYOSHI-KUN!
HOW'D YOU GET UP THERE!?
お～い
HEEEEY!
YOU LOOK LIKE YOU'RE HAVING *FUN!*
AT LEAST THE WHITE THING DOES!
あ
AH!
SO YOU UNDER-STAND ME NOW?
YEAH.
I GET IT NOW.
AT LEAST WHAT YOU TWO ARE SAYING.
SO IT *IS* MOKONA THAT'S DOING IT.

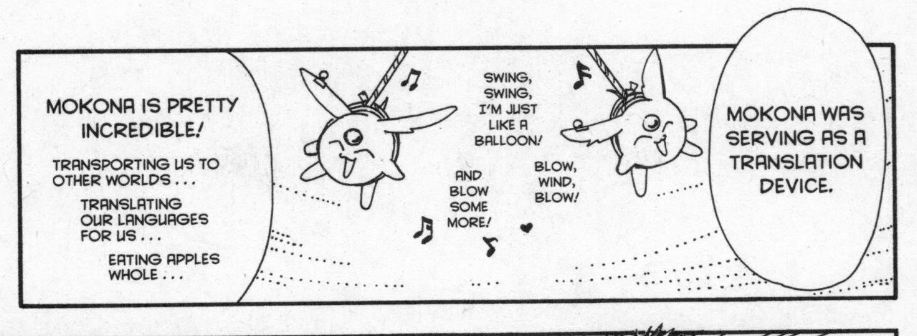
MOKONA WAS SERVING AS A TRANSLATION DEVICE.
BLOW, WIND, BLOW!
SWING, SWING, I'M JUST LIKE A BALLOON!
AND BLOW SOME MORE!
MOKONA IS PRETTY INCREDIBLE!
TRANSPORTING US TO OTHER WORLDS . . .
TRANSLATING OUR LANGUAGES FOR US . . .
EATING APPLES WHOLE . . .

HEY!
DOES THIS MEAN THAT ANY TIME WE GET SEPARATED FROM IT, WE WON'T BE ABLE TO COMMUNI-CATE?
THAT'S WHAT IT MEANS.
TMP
AWW!
TMP TMP
WHAT A PAIN!!
TMP TMP
TMP TMP
TMP

DOOOM
WHAT'S *WITH* THESE PEOPLE?!
A LOT OF THEM, HUH?
DOOOM
わらわら
CHATTER
CHATTER
CHATTER
WHO IS THE ONE WHO WROTE THIS LETTER?!
BOOOM
THAT WOULD BE ME!! ♪
神城
I'll be
waiting at

YEAAAAAAAAH!
PRIMERA-CHAN!!
WHO IS THIS WOMAN?!
YOU DON'T KNOW PRIMERA-CHAN?!
YOU MUST LIVE UNDER A ROCK!!
BOO!
BOO!
BOO!
BOO!
PRIMERA-CHAN IS OUR IDOL!!
SHE SINGS! SHE DANCES! SHE MODELS! SHE EVEN HAS A MORNING TALK SHOW!
MORE THAN THAT, SHE CONTROLS AN INCREDIBLE KUDAN!
CUTE AND STRONG!
SHE'S THE BEST!!

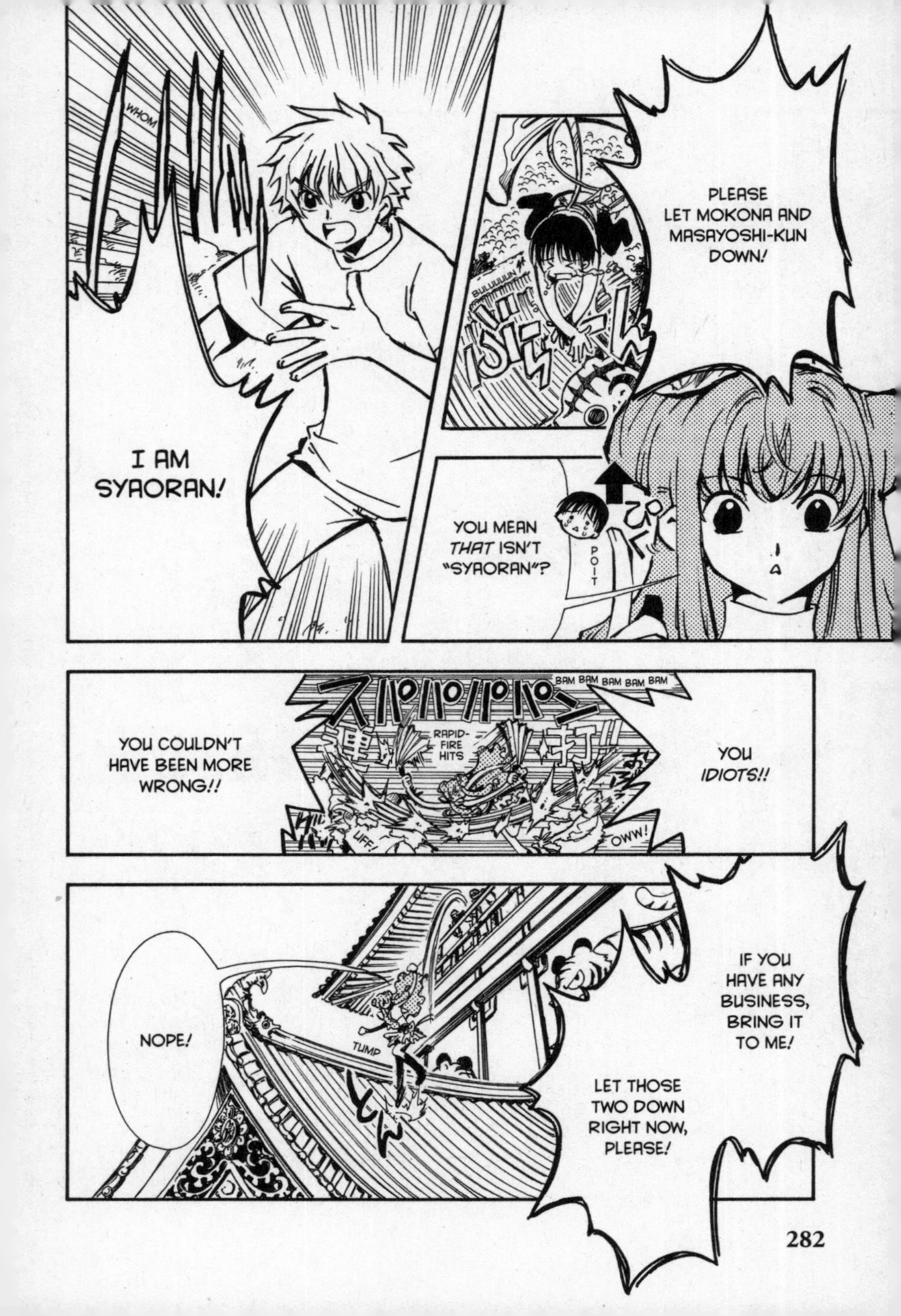
PLEASE LET MOKONA AND MASAYOSHI-KUN DOWN!
BUUUUUUN
WHOM
I AM SYAORAN!
YOU MEAN THAT ISN'T "SYAORAN"?
POIT
BAM BAM BAM BAM BAM
YOU IDIOTS!!
RAPID-FIRE HITS
OWW!
UFF!
YOU COULDN'T HAVE BEEN MORE WRONG!!
IF YOU HAVE ANY BUSINESS, BRING IT TO ME!
LET THOSE TWO DOWN RIGHT NOW, PLEASE!
TUMP
NOPE!

IF YOU WANT THEM BACK, YOU'RE GOING TO HAVE TO *BATTLE* ME FOR THEM!
PRIMERA-CHAN!
YEAAAAAAAAH!
PRIMERA-CHAN!
YEAAAH!
SHE'S SO CUTE!
PRIMERA-CHAN!!
SHE'S SO BEAUTIFUL!
AWW!
SHAD-DAP!
LOVE
WE'LL HAVE TO FIND A WAY UP!
I MIGHT BE ABLE TO GET UP THERE.
YOU KNOW WHERE THE STAIR-CASE IS?
NO...
BUT I SHOULD BE ABLE TO GET THERE.
YEAH?
HOW?
MY KUDAN MAY BE WILLING TO HELP.

HOOWAAAAAA

WAFFF
SUUUU

HWOO
HE'S FLYING!
THESE KUDAN COME IN *EVERY* TYPE.
HUMPH!
MAN!
HE CAN FLY?
NO FAIR!
IF I CAN'T, HE SHOULDN'T BE ALLOWED TO!

MY KUDAN, COME ON!!
SHUULULULU
SHUULULULU
NOW YOU'LL SEE WHAT KIND OF DAMAGE MY KUDAN'S ATTACK CAN DO!
CHINGG
HOO OOM

IS EVERYONE...
...HAVING FUN?! ♪
DMM

BZZT BZZT
IS EVERYONE HAVING FUN?!

DOHOOOM
FAI-
SAN!!

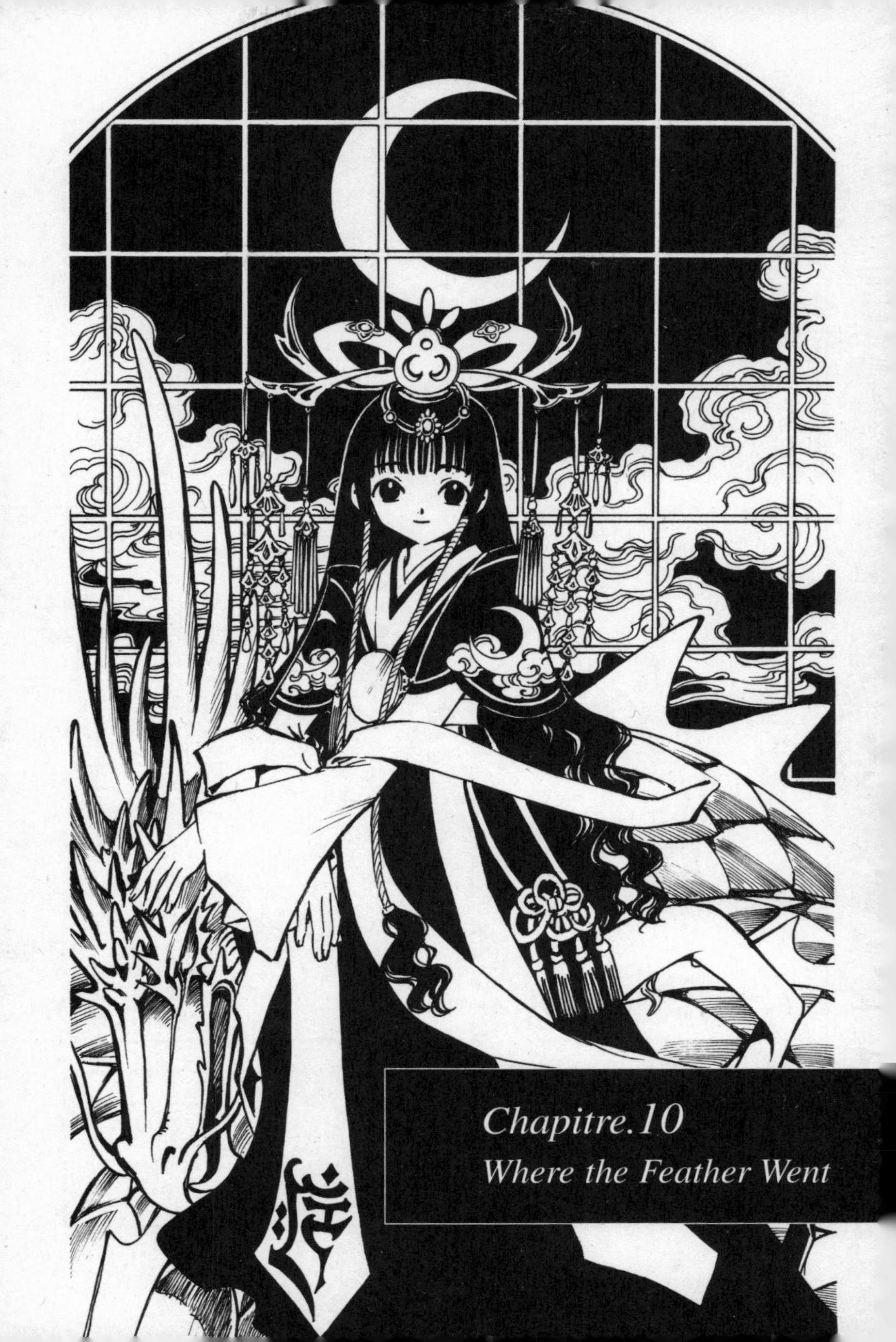
Chapitre.10
Where the Feather Went

SWIP
EH?
LOOK UP THERE.
HUUUUUU
VWAM
THAT WAS A SURPRISE.
A KUDAN CAN DO THAT?
THIS COUNTRY IS PRETTY AMAZING.
YOU LIKED THAT ATTACK, DIDN'T YOU, MOKONA?

CLAP CLAP
AMAZING!
AMAZING!
WAAAAH!
PRIMERA-CHAN'S KUDAN IS SPECIAL LEVEL!
BE CAREFUL!

THAT MAKES ME SO FRUSTRATED!
GRR
WAVE WAVE
GRRR
BUT...
YOU WON'T BEAT ME!!
VWO OM
DOWHOOM
DON'T YOU FLY ON ME!
NO AVOIDING ME EITHER!
DOOOM

BOOOM
QUIT RUNNING AWAY!!
WHY?
WHY CAN'T I *HIT* YOU?
WAFT

IF I LET YOU HIT ME, IT MIGHT HURT.
HENH
GRR
YAAAH!
YAAAH!
GLANCE GLANCE
WHAT ARE YOU PLAN-NING?
YAAAH!
WE HAVE TO GET TO THE TOP AND GET THOSE TWO DOWN!
WE ALSO HAVE TO HELP FAI-SAN!
YOU CAN LEAVE *HIM* ALONE.
HE'LL BE FINE!
HMPH
BAAAM
A TUDOR WHO TOOTED A *FRUIT* TRIED TO TUTOR TWO *DOODOOS* TO TOOT!

KAM
KAM
KAM
KAM
POK
KAM
miss
miss
miss
THE SIXTH SHEIK'S SICKO'S SHIP'S SUNK!
miss
BAAM
I'VE FOUGHT WITH KUDAN, SO I KNOW.
EVEN IF YOUR KUDAN IS ABLE TO FLY, YOUR MUSCLES ARE YOUR BODY'S NORMAL MUSCLES.
PRIMERA-CHAN!!
EVEN HER MISTAKES ARE CUTE!
BBBOOM
YOU MEAN THE ABILITY TO FLOAT AND DODGE LIKE HE'S AS LIGHT AS PAPER... IS FAI-SAN'S OWN ABILITY?
POK
RED LORRY, YELLOW LORRY, RED LORRY, YELLOW YORRY!
PAP
PAP
PAP
PAP
AH.
A FLEA AND A FLY FLEW UP IN A FLUE, EE-AI-EE-AI-OH!

BBB BOOM
LOOK AT THAT DAMN GRIN!
THAT MAN IS A COMBAT VETERAN.
I IMAGINE SO.
BBOOM
EH ?!
THAT DOESN'T SURPRISE YOU?
YEAAAH!
YEAAAH!
THERE'S A CLUE IN THE CASUAL WAY FAI-SAN CARRIES HIMSELF...
...AND ...
...THE LOOK IN HIS EYES JUST GIVES YOU THAT IMPRESSION.
....

MAYBE YOU'RE *NOT* A COMPLETE FOOL.
BUT...I'D STILL LIKE TO HELP HIM OUT IF I CAN.
PRIMERA-CHAN!!
YEAAAH!
¡YEAAAH!
BUT...
I'M RIGHT ABOUT YOU BEING A NAIVE KID!
YEAAAH!
YEAAAH!
YOU FORCED ME INTO IT! *CHANGE!!*
PRIMERA! PRIMERA!
WOOOOOW!!
LOVE

MY KUDAN, CHANGE FORM!!
ZLUUMMM
VWAMM
WHEN MY KUDAN-CHAN BECOMES A MIKE STAND...
...THERE'S NO RUNNING AWAY!
ZWEEEEEEEN
ALL THE FANS LOVE MEEEEEEE...

ZWOOM
...EEEEEEEEEEEEEEE...
ZLIP
HEH!
...EE-YEAH!

ZWOOOM

KAKK
FAI-
SAN!!
BBOOOM
SHHH
FAI-
SAN!!
SHHH
I'M ALL
RIGHT!
SHAKK

I NEVER EXPECTED IT TO CHANGE FORM!
AND THOSE LETTERS SURE COME AFTER YOU!
PAT PAT
AND SINCE THIS GIRL IS FIGHTING WITH HER KUDAN, AND MOKONA ISN'T REACTING...
...IT MUST MEAN THAT THE GIRL ISN'T THE ONE WITH THE FEATHER.
TWIRL, TWIRL. I'M JUST LIKE A WATER BALLOON!
WHIRL, WHIRL.
SNIFF SNIFF
AH HA HA!
WELL?
DO YOU SURRENDER?
YEAH! YEAH!
IF I DID, WHAT WOULD HAPPEN NEXT?
THEN I MOVE ON TO THE NEXT ONE TO DEFEAT, THIS "SYAORAN" GUY!
WE CAN'T HAVE THAT.
SYAORAN-KUN HAS SOME IMPORTANT BUSINESS TO SEE THROUGH.

I'D REALLY RATHER THAT IT ENDS WITH ME.
YEAAH!
YEAAH!
YEAAH!
PRIMERA-CHAN!
PRIMERA-CHAN!
HEH
IF SO...
...THEN I...

WILL JUST HAVE TO WIIIIIIIIN!!
GWOOO
SWUP
THUMP

TMP
TMP
TMP
TMP
TMP
TMP
EH?!

I DON'T WANT TO BE THE CAUSE OF INJURY TO A BEAUTIFUL YOUNG WOMAN.
WON'T YOU STOP?
DAA

SNIFF
TH—
THIS IS SO NOT FAIR!!
B- B- BWOM
B-BOOM
AH!!
WHEEE!
HYUUUUUN
WAAAAAH!

SHUUUUU
OH NO!
WATCH OUT!!
FWOMM
BAMP

WHAT DO YOU THINK YOU'RE *DOING*, PRIMERA?
SHÔGO-KUN!
BOINK

Chapitre.11
The Kudan of Fire

ツバサ
RESERVoir CHRoNiCLE

YOU'VE GOT WORK TO DO, RIGHT?
YOU'RE AN IDOL, RIGHT?
DON'T YOU HAVE A CONCERT TO PREPARE FOR?
HMPH!
IT'S THAT LEADER FROM BEFORE!
I DID IT BECAUSE ... BECAUSE *YOU* NEVER COME TO SEE ME!
YOU DON'T! YOU DON'T!
THANK YOU
BESIDES, THERE'S *PLENTY* OF TIME!
THE CONCERT'S AT THE HANSHIN DOME RIGHT OVER THERE!
EVEN IF IT IS ...
WHY ARE YOU DESTROYING OUR CULTURAL HERITAGE?!
DON'T BLAME *ME* IF THEY GET ALL MAD OVER IT!

YOU BREAK BUILDINGS ALL THE TIME, SHÔGO-KUN! DON'T TALK TO *ME* ALL HIGH AND MIGHTY!
WHAT WAS THAT?!
なにぃっ!!

WHAT ARE THESE TWO SQUABBLING ABOUT?
HUH?
あー?
WAFT
UH?
UH?

SNFFL
うっ
SNFFL
うっ
SNFFL
うっ
L O V E
SNFFL
うっ
SNFFL
うっ
SNFFL
うっ

HM?
WHAT ARE YOU ALL CRYING OVER?
WAAAAH!
うわああん

PRIMERA-CHAN'S IN LOVE WITH THAT TEAM LEADER, THERE!
PRIMERA-CHAN!
プリメーラちゃーん
BUT ...
...SINCE HE NEVER COMES TO SEE HER, SHE'S LONELY!!
WAAAAAH!

HOW DO YOU KNOW?
WHO WOULD YOU MOST LIKE TO BE WITH?
On Your Days Off
BECAUSE PRIMERA-CHAN MADE IT OFFICIAL!
WARAAAAH!
PRIMERA-CHAN!!
PAK
SEE FOR YOUR-SELF!
VWOOSH
でも可愛いんだよーっ!!
BUT SHE'S SOOO CUTE!!
AARE
STAR
YOU'RE LOOKING IN THE WRONG PLACE! LOOK AT THE PHOTO SPREAD IN FRONT !!
WEEKLY
25
TORA WATER
WAAAAAAH!!

I HEAR THAT THERE'S SOME TERRITORIAL RUMBLE GOING ON, SO I COME TO SEE WHAT'S UP, AND ...
FOOOM
I WAS IN THE MIDDLE OF A DELIVERY!
I DON'T KNOW ABOUT YOU, BUT *I'M* SUPPOSED TO GO TO SCHOOL AND HELP OUT WITH THE FAMILY BUSINESS!
WE'RE RIGHT DOWN THE STREET!
YOU KNOW THE ADDRESS!
ASAGI LIQUORS
浅黄酒店
WAAH!
BUT I'M *LONELY!!*
っていうか
THEY LOOK ...
違うし
... NOTHING ALIKE!
YOU'RE SO DUMB!
WAAAAAAAH!!
ぴょん
BOING
UM ...
SO I ASKED THIS GUY YOU LIKE OVER TO SEE ME, HOPING HE WOULD JOIN THE PRIMERA FAN CLUB, AND WHILE YOU VISITED WITH HIM, YOU COULD SEE *ME*, TOO!

SYAORAN!
SYAORAN!
MOKONA!
YOUR EYES!!
ぴょん
BOING
ぴょん
BOING
BOING
IT'S HERE!
THE FEATHER IS REAL CLOSE BY!
WHERE?
WHO HAS IT?!
ぴょん
BOING
ぴょん
BOING
MOKONA DOESN'T KNOW!
BUT MOKONA JUST FELT A HUGE WAVE!

SO SOME KUDAN HAS TAKEN IT INSIDE ITSELF.
BUT...
...IT GETS STRONGER AND THEN GETS WEAKER.
WHAT IS THAT SUPPOSED TO MEAN?
WHY ISN'T IT ONE FIXED STRENGTH?

SORATA-SAN SAID THAT KUDAN PROTECT THEIR OWNERS.
SO PROBABLY, THE TIME THAT IT PUTS OUT ITS GREATEST STRENGTH IS WHEN IT'S PROTECTING ITS OWNER.

DOOOM
AND THAT MEANS...
...THE WAY TO FIND THE FEATHER IS THROUGH BATTLE!

I'M SORRY THAT MY WORDS CAUSED UN-EXPECTED TROUBLE FOR YOU...
...SYAORAN.
BUT I MEANT IT. I DO LIKE YOUR STYLE.
YOU'RE STRONG.
AND BY THAT, I DON'T MEAN YOU GOT MUSCLES. RIGHT HERE.
HEH
THUMP
SO I WANTED TO TRY TO TAKE YOU ON...
...WITH OUR KUDAN.
SHÔGO-KUN, ALL YOU CARE ABOUT ARE YOUR KUDAN BATTLES! YOU RETARD!
DON'T SAY "RETARD"!
CALL ME A "FOOL" OR AN "IDIOT" IF YOU LIKE.
I UNDER-STAND.
SST
PFF

THEN I ACCEPT...
...YOUR CHALLENGE!

SHHK
YOU GUYS, STAY OUTTA THIS, GOT ME?
FOWOOO!!
I BET 3000 KO ON SHÔGO!
I GOT MY MONEY ON SYRORAN!
2000 KO!!

LIKE I SAID IN MY DREAM, I WANT POWER.
POWER TO PROTECT SAKURA.
READY!
YOU'LL FIGHT ALONG-SIDE ME?
SSS
YEAAH!
YEAAH!
YEAAH!
SSHAA

GO!!
WHOOM

KRMBLE
KRMBLE
TMP
WATCH OUT!!
WAA
HOOM

WHEEET-WHOOO!
HE'S PRETTY COOL... ...SYAORAN-KUN.
SO HE'S MORE THAN JUST A PLIABLE FOOL.
YOU BOTH HAVE FACES THAT SAY, "IGNORE ME, I'M A FOOL!" BUT I SEE THROUGH IT.
YEAH.
IT SEEMS LIKE HE'S MORE THAN A GUY WITH AN ARCHAEOLOGY HOBBY.
HE'S STILL VERY YOUNG...
...BUT YOUNG PEOPLE CAN COME THROUGH THEIR PAIN.
AND I BELIEVE HE HAS.

MOKONA!
CAN YOU FEEL THE FEATHER'S WAVE?
SHHT
THE WAVE *IS* THERE, BUT MOKONA DOESN'T KNOW WHO HAS IT!
NO NO NO
I GUESS WE WON'T KNOW UNTIL WE MAKE THE WAVE BIGGER.
I DON'T KNOW IF *THAT* KUDAN IS THE ONE WITH THE FEATHER...
...BUT THERE'S NO DOUBT THAT IT HAS TO BE A STRONG KUDAN!
AND I HAVE TO MAKE SURE!!

SAKURA'S
FEATHER
IS CLOSE
BY!!

GWOO

KAM
KAM
KAM
KAM
KAM
DOOOM
SHÔGO-
KUN!!

FWA SOOM
PLIP
PLIP
OH, MAN!
THAT WAS THE FIRST TIME I WAS EVER HIT LIKE THAT!
TUMP
SHÔGO-KUN!!
I'M FINE!
I TOLD YOU TO STOP SCREAMING MY NAME!
YOU'LL RUIN YOUR VOICE JUST BEFORE A CONCERT!
WH— WHO EVER SAID I CARED WHAT HAPPENS TO YOU?!
WHSSH
WHSSH
DON'T TALK SO BIG! YOU'RE BREAKING STUFF TOO!
SHE'S SO CUTE!
CHATTER
CHATTER

REALLY!
YOU'RE A TOUGH ONE.
KUDAN ARE CON-TROLLED BY THE HEART.
WHAT IS IT THAT MAKES YOURS SO STRONG?
I HAVE SOMETHING THAT I *MUST* SEE THROUGH.
THAT MAKES SENSE.

EVERYONE, GET OUTTA HERE!!
FAM
FOWOOO
SET!
GO!!
SHAAAAA
GWOOO

DOOOOOOOOM

KYAA!
KYAA!
GMMMMMMMM
ZLUUU

SYAORAN-KUN!!

THIS IS TERRIBLE!!
SHAAAAAHH
SYAORAN-KUN WILL GET WASHED AWAY!!
I HAVE TO FIND HIM!
WHERE?
WHERE?
SHUUU
SHHHHHHHHHH
EH?!
SYAORAN IS RIGHT THERE!

DOOM

AMAZING...
へたん
SLUMP
HE SAID HE CAME FROM A FOREIGN COUNTRY...
BUT JUST LOOK AT THE WAY HE CONTROLS HIS KUDAN!
GRMP
ME TOO!
I WANT TO BE STRONG, TOO!

JUST LIKE HIM!
SHHHHHHHH
STRONG!
KNCH
KNCH

RMMBL
RMMBL
WATCH OUT!!
GAGARASSH
KYAAAAAH!!
NO!
I CAN'T LEAVE JUST TO SAVE MYSELF!
WHOO
NOT WHEN THERE ARE PEOPLE TO PROTECT!!

I HAVE
TO BE
STRONG
!!!
KAKK

zwuuuuuuuuuu

BOINK
WHAAAA??
CLATTR
CLATTR
MOKONA FOUND IT!
THE FEATHER!
IT'S IN THAT KUDAN!!

Chapitre.12
The Proof of Bravery

DID I HEAR RIGHT?
THE FEATHER'S IN THAT KUDAN?
IN *THAT* KUDAN?!
RMMMM
I THINK I SEE... EVEN WHEN HE USED HIS KUDAN TO FIND US, MOKONA DIDN'T DETECT IT.
BUT WHEN IT PROTECTS ITS MASTER...
THE TIME WHEN IT NEEDS THE MOST POWER IS WHEN IT IS PROTECTING SOMEONE IT CARES ABOUT FROM A LIFE-OR-DEATH SITUATION.

THE LAST TIME MOKONA DETECTED IT...
...WAS ALSO WHEN MASAYOSHI WAS IN A DANGEROUS SITUATION.
KRAKL
KRAKL
WAAAA!
YOU JUST PUT THAT BOY DOWN RIGHT NOW!
BATTA
BATTA
EVEN NOW, IT'S TRYING TO PROTECT HIM FROM THE CRUMBLING CASTLE.
SHOOOO

WOOOOO
SAKURA'S FEATHER...
...IS INSIDE THAT!

KYOOOOOO
KYAAAAAAH!!
KRATTR
KRATTR
プリメーラちゃん!!
PRIMERA-CHAN!!

KASH
SHÔGO-KUN!
WAAAAH!
THERE, THERE
PHEW!
I WAS SO SCARED!!
MOKONA, TOO!!
HUGG
THAT THING EVEN STARTLED *ME!*
I MEAN, THAT KUDAN IS *BIG!*
HUGG
ZHOON
KRAKK

KWOOOM
H-HEY, I'M ALL RIGHT!
I'M JUST FINE!
GO BACK TO *NORMAL* ALREADY!

DOOOM
WHAT'S WRONG WITH THAT KUDAN?
DOOOM
THE FEATHER HAD TOO MUCH POWER FOR IT.
THAT'S MORE KUDAN THAN MASA-YOSHI CAN CONTROL.
WAFFT

STOP IT!!
WHAT'LL YOU DO NOW?
SHHP

I'M GOING TO GET SAKURA'S FEATHER BACK.
HOW DO YOU INTEND TO FIGHT SOMETHING THAT BIG?
ONE SLIP UP AND YOU'RE DEAD!
I WON'T DIE.

I STILL HAVE SOME-THING TO SEE THROUGH.
I CAN'T DIE YET.

MM.
COUNT ON KURO-PI TO HANDLE THINGS HERE.
YOU GO AHEAD.
EH?!
WHAT DO YOU MEAN, ME?!
THEN I'LL SEE YOU LATER.

WHOOSH
SYAORAN-KUN HAS STRENGTH.
IN A LOT OF DIFFERENT WAYS.

I GET THE FEELING THAT I UNDERSTAND...
DOOOM
...WHY THAT FIRE KUDAN CAME TO HIM.

STOP!!
I TOLD YOU TO STOP!!
GWOOOO

GLTTR
GLTTR
IT'S SPARKLING.

WOBBL
D-DOOM
DOOM
GASP
TMP
SYAORAN-KUN!!

I TOLD YOU THAT THERE WAS SOME-THING I WAS LOOKING FOR.
Y—
YOU MEAN THIS?!
WHOOM
NOW ...
...I'VE FOUND IT INSIDE OF YOUR KUDAN.
I NEED TO GET IT BACK.

BUT...
MY KUDAN ISN'T LISTENING TO A WORD I SAY!
WHOOOSH
SYAORAN-KUN!
IF YOU GET TOO CLOSE, IT'LL–
ZUWHOOM

GUGURK
GHOOOOOH
MY KUDAN IS SPOUTING FIRE!!
STOP IT!!
YOU'LL KILL SYAORAN-KUN!!

ZHUUUUUUUUU
SHUU
SHUU
ZLOOB
ZLOOB
YOU'LL KILL SYAORAN-KUN!
YOU'LL KILL HIM!!

SYAORAN-KUN!
FWAAA
SYAORAN-KUN!
H-HOT!!
AH!

GHOOOOH
MASAYOSHI-KUN!
URRNG!
T—
TAKE IT!!
IF THE THING INSIDE MY KUDAN IS THE THING YOU'RE LOOKING FOR...
...THEN I WANT YOU TO HAVE IT!
KRKL
KRKL

SO IF IT BURNS ME, LET IT BURN!!

ZUUZUUM
PLEASE...
TAKE IT!!

SHUULUUULUULUUM
KWOOO
SHHHHHH
SHÔGO'S KUDAN!
PLIP
PLIP
TUMP

SHHHHHHHHHH
THE *LEAST* I COULD DO WAS KEEP THE PLACE FROM CATCHING FIRE.

PARA
SAKURA'S FEATHER!
SAKURA'S MEMORY!
I WAS ABLE...
...TO GET ONE BACK FOR HER!

Chapitre.13
The Reason for Tears

IT'S GOTTEN CLOUDY.
I WONDER IF IT'LL TURN INTO A SHOWER.
TMP TMP TMP
WELCOME HOME, SYAORAN!
HOW'D IT GO?
WAZZAT?
TWRL
TMP
I SEE YOU'RE IN SOMETHING OF A HURRY.
BUT WHY DO YOU LOOK LIKE A DIRTY CINDER?
I FOUND ONE OF SAKURA'S FEATHERS!
YOU DID?!

BAKAM
PAAAAAA
WITH THIS FEATHER... PLEASE WAKE UP!
SAKURA!!

"IF I FALL ASLEEP LIKE THIS..."
"...THE FIRST THING I'LL SEE WHEN I WAKE UP..."
PAAA
"...WILL BE YOU, SYAORAN."
GRMP

MNN
SAKURA!!

.....
WHO...

...ARE YOU?

I'M CALLED SYAORAN.
AND YOU...
...ARE HER HIGHNESS, PRINCESS SAKURA.

IF YOU'D BE SO KIND AS TO LISTEN, I'LL EXPLAIN.
YOU ARE A PRINCESS FROM ANOTHER WORLD.
ANOTHER... WORLD?
AND AT THE MOMENT, YOU'VE LOST YOUR MEMORY. IT'S IN ORDER TO FIND YOUR MEMORIES THAT YOU'RE TRAVELING BETWEEN WORLDS.
PAK
PAK

BY MYSELF?
NO...
YOU HAVE TRAVELING COMPANIONS.
ARE YOU... ONE OF THOSE?
YES.

YOU'RE DOING THIS FOR A TOTAL STRANGER?
I AM.
PRINCESS SAKURA, I'M PLEASED TO MAKE YOUR ACQUAINTANCE.
FAI D. FLOWRIGHT AT YOUR SERVICE.
SST
DMP

AND MAY I PRESENT—
I'M KURO-GANE.

AND THIS CUTE, FLUFFY ONE IS...
SHUPP
MOKONA MODOKI! BUT YOU CAN SAY MOKONA!

NICE TA MEETCHA!
SHAKE!

SHHHHHHHHHHHHHHH

AT THAT MOMENT, I WAS SURE...
...HE WOULD CRY.
IT SEEMS THAT SAKURA-CHAN IS THE MOST IMPORTANT PERSON IN THE WORLD TO SYAORAN-KUN.
SO WHEN SHE SAID, "WHO ARE YOU?" I FELT CERTAIN HE WOULD CRY.
I WONDER IF HE'S CRYING NOW.
DON'T KNOW.
BUT IF HE WANTS TO KEEP FROM CRYING, HE'LL JUST HAVE TO GET STRONGER.
STRONG ENOUGH SO THAT *HE* WON'T BE THE ONE CRYING IN THE END.

YEAH...
PWAFF
BUT...
I ALSO THINK THERE'S A CERTAIN STRENGTH THAT'S NEEDED TO BE ABLE TO CRY WHEN YOU SHOULD.

WHILE I WAS SLEEPING, I WONDER IF SOME-ONE WAS HOLDING MY HAND...
MY HAND...
...FELT JUST SO NICE AND WARM!

IT SEEMS ONE OF THE FEATHERS HAS BEEN RETURNED TO HER.
YES.
BUT IN THE PATHS TO COME, THERE IS NO GUARANTEE THAT THEY WILL BE AS LUCKY AS THEY WERE THIS TIME.

THE POWER TO SPAN DIMEN-SIONS . . .
. . . WILL FALL INTO MY HANDS . . .

...NO MATTER HOW MUCH BLOOD NEEDS TO SPILL TO MAKE IT HAPPEN!

Past Works

CLAMP have created many series. Here is a brief overview of one of them.

X/1999

Kamui Shirou left Tokyo after the death of the mother of his friends, Fuma and Kotori. Now, six years later, Kamui is confronted by a vision of his own mother's death. Burning, she commands him to seek his destiny in Tokyo, and so he returns.

A turning point for the planet Earth is coming in the year 1999. Ravaged by mankind's carelessness, the planet is polluted and near death. The priestess Hinoto has seen two possible visions for humanity: In one, mankind is saved, and in the other, mankind is destroyed so that the earth can be born anew. The Seven Seals, or Dragons of Heaven, are pledged to fight for the preservation of humanity. The Seven Minions, or Dragons of Earth, want to exterminate all human life to make way for a new age.

Hinoto's vision centers on Kamui, who has the power to choose the world's fate. Pledged to protect his childhood friends Fuma and Kotori, Kamui finds allies in the form of Arashi and Sorata, two of the Seven Seals. (You've already met the Hanshin-reality versions of Arashi and Sorata (Sora) in *Tsubasa* volume 1.) For the sake of his friends, Kamui chooses to fight for the Seven Seals. Sadly, Fuma is Kamui's "twin star," his opposite number, and because Kamui chose the side of good for himself, Fuma is forced to join the side of evil, the Seven Minions. Thus Kamui must fight the friend he sought to save.

Acknowledged as one of CLAMP's most visually stunning manga, *X/1999* is set in the same world as *CLAMP School Detectives* and *Tokyo Babylon*, and is still an ongoing series. The manga has been adapted as an anime film and a TV series.

Translation Notes

Japanese is a tricky language for most Westerners, and translation is often more art than science. For your edification and reading pleasure, here are notes on some of the places where we could have gone in a different direction in our translation of the work, or where a Japanese cultural reference is used.

Kyaa!
"Kyaaaa" is standard onomatopoeia (sound word) for a scream in manga, but many Japanese people have adopted this sound and use it to express joy, surprise, and other happy emotions.

Tsuruhashi
The town in which our heroes stop by to eat okonomiyaki (see next entry) is called Tsuruhashi. In our world, Tsuruhashi is only about a kilometer south of Osaka Castle, and it is the station which connects the Osaka Loop Line that circles the city, with the Kintetsu-Nara line, which goes out to the suburbs between Osaka and Nara. Millions of people pass through this station, and because of that, it's only natural that the restaurants there are both famous and good!

Okonomiyaki

They call it Japanese pancakes or Japanese pizza, but the only thing similar between those and okonomiyaki is that all are round and flat. Okonomiyaki is made of flour, water, cabbage (mixed with other veggies), egg, seasonings, some kind of meat (seafood is common), and a delicious steak-sauce-like okonomiyaki sauce. The "konomi" means "like" or "love," and it indicates that you can put the veggies or meat you most like in it. The "yaki" means fried (the same as with "teriyaki" or "sukiyaki").

Flipping Rights

Most okonomiyaki that you will find in Japan is made in the kitchen, or at least, behind the counter. However, there are okonomiyaki restaurants where you can flip the okonomiyaki yourself. But since the dish was created in the Kansai (Osaka, Kyoto, Nara, Kobe) region, chefs jealously guard the right to flip their okonomiyaki—only when it's ready. After all, they are proud of their food and want it to be perfectly cooked.

KANI-NABE SENKAI!*

Attack Names

Most anime, manga, and game fans are familiar with the attack names that the opponents shout at each other when making their attacks. Sure, it doesn't happen in real life, but it is a long-time entertainment convention. CLAMP was having a little crabby fun with the names of the attacks in this sequence.

Kuro-tan

The pet names that Fai always chooses for Kurogane aren't actually honorifics. Although they are similar in meaning to -chan, they are usually invented by young women who want to appear cute and add cute sounds to the names of people in their inner circle (close female friends and boyfriends). These syllables make the name sound almost babylike, and so Fai giving those names to gruff Kurogane is massively inappropriate, and as such, very funny.

Drawbacks to Hanshin's People

Sorata's list of complaints about the people of the Hanshin Republic are common conceptions that Tokyoites have for the people of Osaka. Their stand-up comedy is famous for a Laurel and Hardy dynamic where one person says something dumb, and the other hits him over the head for it. And yes, they do throw themselves into the dirty, polluted river when the Hanshin Tigers win the national championship.

Kurogane's Language

Students of Chinese or Japanese may be able to make some sense out of Kurogane's language. The kanji in his word balloons are real, and if you look them up, you should be able to get some idea of what he is saying.

We Have a Winner!

The original sound effect here was "Pin-pon, pin-pon," the universal sound (in Japan) for a correct answer in a quiz show.

Primera's Legion of Fans

Yes, CLAMP's depiction of Primera's fans is an exaggeration, but not by all that much...

"Is Everyone Having Fun?"

The Japanese phrase here is actually "Minna genki?" Similar to "Hello, Cleveland!" this is a standard phrase for a singer to say as a concert is beginning.

Tongue Twister 1

Like English, Japanese has a large variety of tongue twisters, and here some of the more famous are misquoted by Primera. "Tonari no Kyaku wa yoku kaki kuu kyaku da" ("The guest next door eats a lot of persimmon"). But Primera said, "Tonari no gaki wa yoku kyaku kuu gaki da" ("The brat next door eats a lot of guests").

Tongue Twister 2

The tongue twister Primera wanted to say was, "Nama-mugi, nama-gome, nama-tamago" ("Raw barley, raw rice, raw egg"), but she got one word wrong. "Nama-gome" became "Nama-gomi" ("Raw garbage").

Tongue Twister 3

Primera tried to say, "Aka maki-gami, ao maki-gami, ki maki-gami" ("Red rolled paper, blue rolled paper, yellow rolled paper"), but she stumbled over the last words so it came out, "Maki-maki" ("rolled rolled").

RED LORRY, YELLOW LORRY, RED LORRY, YELLOW *YORRY!*

Tongue Twister 4

Primera was out of tongue twisters at this point, and she just started stringing words together like "pond skater," "red," and "aeiou."

A FLEA AND A FLY FLEW UP IN A FLUE, EE-AI-EE-AI-OH!

"Call me idiot!"

The word for fool, "baka," that many fans know already, is Tokyo dialect. A different word for fool, "aho," is Osaka dialect. Oddly, "aho" is not terribly insulting in Osaka, but "baka" is, and the opposite is true in Tokyo. In the Japanese version, Primera called Shôgo "baka," and Shôgo replied, "At least say, 'Aho'!" He was noting that Primera was getting away from her Hanshin roots by using the word "baka."

Tsubasa Volume 3 Contents

RESERVoir CHRoNiCLE
TSUBASA

ツバサ
RESERVoir CHRoNiCLE

Chapitre.14
Time to Get Under Way

HSSSHHH
HSSSHHH
BOTH MY KUDAN AND I...
...WERE ALWAYS SO WEAK, SO...
MNCH
MNCH
MASA-YOSHI-KUN...
...I REALLY WANT TO THANK YOU.
EH HEH HEH
THAT ONE'S MINE!
SO...
PINNT
SO...
I'M GLAD YOU WERE ABLE TO GET THE FEATHER!

YOU AREN'T WEAK!
STRENGTH AND WEAKNESS AREN'T MEASURED ONLY IN BATTLE.
GOING OUT AND DOING YOUR BEST FOR SOMEONE ELSE'S SAKE...
...IS A WONDERFUL SIGN OF STRENGTH.

GWI
THANKS!
THANK YOU!

YO.
SHÔGO-SAN!!
EH?!
HM?
AHHH!
POK
HUH?

I'M GLAD MY TEAM GETS GOOD INTELLIGENCE.
CAN YOU SKOOCH OVER A BIT?
'SCUSE ME, WE'RE READY TO ORDER. I'LL HAVE TONPEI-YAKI!
HM?!!

OH! IT'S BEGINNING TO BURN. YOU'D BETTER EAT IT.
I'LL HAVE FUTA-MODAN.
AND A TORA-COLA.
OF COURSE, SIR.
OKAY!
STAAARE
MNCHA
MNCHA

ONE FUTA-MODAN FOR THIS GENTLEMAN, YOUR MAJESTY!
YOUR MAJESTY?!
STAAARE
YOUR MAJESTY, REALLY?!
YOUR MAJESTY?!
I TOLD YOU TO STOP THAT!!

NOBODY GOT WOUNDED, RIGHT?
WE'RE FINE.

I'M SORRY TO HAVE INTERRUPTED YOUR BATTLE.
ぺこり
BOW
YAAAAAH!
IT'S OKAY.
IT WAS THE ONLY THING YOU COULD DO, CIRCUM-STANCES BEING WHAT THEY WERE.
BOINK

BESIDES, I WAS LOSING THAT BATTLE BADLY.

BOOO!
BOOO!
BOOO!
BOOO!
BOOO!
I LOST 3000 TORA ON THAT!
I WON!
OH, SHUT UP!
うるせー

HOW LONG WILL YOU BE IN THE HANSHIN REPUBLIC?

WE'LL HAVE TO GO TO A NEW WORLD... ERR... COUNTRY VERY SOON.
I SEE...
YOU LITTLE SLUG!
YOU STOLE MY FOOD AGAIN!
KUROGANE IS TERRIBLE! HE MADE MOKONA GO "BOINK" FROM THE HEAT!
MOKONA, I THINK YOUR TAIL IS A LITTLE BURNT.
GRRRND

I'D HOPED TO MEET YOU IN OTHER PLACES THAN JUST BATTLE.
I WANTED TO GUIDE YOU AROUND TOWN A BIT.
PRIMERA WAS DISAPPOINTED, TOO.

SST

GLNCH

IF WE MAKE IT BACK HERE, WE'LL LOOK YOU UP.
COUNT ON IT!
FoWoooo!
TAKE CARE!!

NOW...
I'VE GOT ONE LAST QUESTION TO ASK.
?!
ZWIP
HEH
JOIN UP.
BE A PART OF MY TEAM.
I...

I SURE WILL!!

わっ
YEAH!!
じっ
STARE
紀伊國屋書

わしゃわしゃ
NOOGIE NOOGIE

鶴橋

YOU'RE GOING ALREADY?
YES.
BUT YOU HAVEN'T TASTED ALL OF THE COOKING THAT'S GENERATED THROUGH THE LOVE OF MY HONEY AND MYSELF!
GRN!
THANK YOU SO MUCH!
BOUGHT THIS, TOO.
ARE YOU ALL RIGHT?
RUBB
I'M STILL A LITTLE SLEEPY.

DON'T LOOK DOWN.
IF YOU ARE A MAN WHO HAS A JOB TO DO...
...YOU ALWAYS HAVE TO LOOK AHEAD!
ALL RIGHT.

FAZAA
THANK YOU SO MUCH FOR EVERYTHING!
PAAAAA
FOR WHAT?
WE DIDN'T DO ANYTHING SPECIAL.
I PRAY THAT YOU FIND ONE OF SAKURA'S FEATHERS IN YOUR NEXT WORLD.

GWAAAHH
SHU
LOOM
SO THOSE WERE THE ONES THAT YÛKO-SAN WAS COUNTING ON.
YOU KNOW, I THINK THEY CAN OVER-COME ANY HARDSHIP THEY MAY FIND.
YES.
かに道
風月

GOWAAAAAA
THANK YOU!

GOWRRRRRR
WHAT'S THIS?
A LOT OF PEOPLE THERE!
GABASSH

カルラッ
KRMBL
GLANCE
ギョ

WOW!
I THINK WE'RE THE CENTER OF ATTENTION!
HUH?
WHAT IS IT NOW?
HEY!
HEY!
EH HEH!
SHULOOM
EVERYBODY WANTS TO SEE MOKONA!!
HERE WE ARE IN ANOTHER WEIRD PLACE!
WHO THE HELL ARE THEY?!
SHKK
AND WHERE DID YOU COME FROM?!
GRABB

SHA-KOW

OH!
AH HA!
WHEE! ♡

SKREEEEECH
TONK
JUST WHO DO YOU THINK YOU'RE KICKING IN THE FACE?!
SHAK
SHAK
DOOM
STOP RIGHT THERE !!

Chapitre.15
The Secret Country

IF YOU DON'T WANT TO BE KICKED, DON'T GO ATTACKING PEOPLE AT RANDOM!
YOU STUPID LITTLE BOY!!
DOOM
A GIRL!
BLIP
CHU'NYAN!!

WHO ARE YOU CALLING STUPID?!
GLANCE キョロ キョロ GLANCE
GRRRR
I DON'T SEE ANYBODY STUPIDER THAN YOU.
ぶるぶるぶる ぶる
GRWL GRWL GRWL GRWL
YOU LITTLE...
YOU INSULT ME?!
I AM THE ONLY SON OF THE RYANBAN-SAMA, THE MASTER OF THE COUNTRY OF KORYO *INCLUDING* THE TOWN OF RYONFI!

YOU MAY *CALL* HIM RYAN-BAN ...
...BUT LESS THAN A YEAR AGO, HE WAS JUST A WANDERING SHINBAN MAGICIAN!

KRAA
YOU DARE PUT DOWN MY FATHER?!
DO YOU KNOW THE PUNISHMENT FOR OPPOSING THE RYANBAN?!
CHU'NYAN?!
GNCH

GRUMBLE
GRUMBLE
I CLAIM THE RIGHT OF RETRIBUTION FOR THESE INSULTS!
JUST BE PREPARED!
ARE YOU HURT?
I'M JUST FINE.
SHMP
SHMP
THANK YOU!
WELL...
...IT LOOKS LIKE WE MADE A SPLASH IMMEDIATELY AFTER OUR ARRIVAL.
SHMP
SHMP
SYAORAN WAS *GREAT!*
JUMPING AROUND!
WHAT IS ALL THIS?
JMMP

AAH!!
MOKONA WILL HELP TOO!!
THAT WHITE MANJU BUN SPOKE !!
きゃーっ
YAAAH!
COME ON, KURO-PIN, YOU PICK THEM UP, TOO.
SLUMP
SLUMP
AAA! WHAT A PAIN!
STOMP
STOMP
I'M SORRY!
YOU MEANT TO SELL THESE, RIGHT?
ぺこり
BOW

CHATTR
LOOK AT THESE GUYS!
RUNNING AMOK IN OUR MARKET!
CHATTR
POKKA POKKAM

I CAN ONLY WISH THAT AMEN'OSA WOULD COME TO TOWN AS QUICKLY AS THEY CAN.
GRIII

HUH?
KA-THNK
BOING

THOSE ARE WEIRD CLOTHES!
DOOOM
ZU-

AH HA HA
HA HA HA!
SHE CALLED
THEM WEIRD!
SLEEPY ねむねむ
KUROGANE'S WEIRD!
MUST'VE BEEN TALKING ABOUT YOUR CLOTHES, KURO-RIN!
IF I'M WEIRD, THEN SO ARE YOU!!
YOU PEOPLE!
ARE YOU GUYS...

COME WITH ME!
あ! AH!
WAIT A MOMENT!
TMP
WE'RE BUSY RIGHT OFF THE BAT.
SORRY, MISTER!
TMP
TMP
THIS IS *SUCH* A PAIN!
TMP
AW!
KYAA! MOKONA'S FALLING OFF!

じっ
STARE
ちょこん
HUSH
SH
SH

UM... WHERE ARE...
MY HOUSE.
WHY DID YOU SUDDENLY...

DON'T YOU HAVE SOMETHING TO SAY?

HUH??
HUH?
UM... IT'S JUST...
いや・あの
WE ONLY NOW ARRIVED IN YOUR COUNTRY.
WE JUST MET YOU...
DOOOM
YOU DON'T?
YOU REALLY DON'T?
ZLIP
ZLIP
HANG IN THERE, SYAORAN-KUN!
I CAN'T ...
...SAY THAT...
...I DO.
NOW THAT I THINK OF IT, CHILDREN LIKE YOU COULDN'T BE AMEN'OSA, COULD YOU?
はーっ
SIIIIGH
AMEN'OSA?

AMEN'OSA IS A SMALL GROUP OF AGENTS THAT THE GOVERNMENT SENDS AROUND THE COUNTRY.
THEY KNOW THAT SOME OF THE RYANBAN ARE ACTING ONLY IN THEIR OWN SELF INTEREST IN THE REGIONS THEY CONTROL.
THEY KNOW SOME PEOPLE ARE OPPRESSED.
THEY TRAVEL ABOUT THE COUNTRY WITH A MISSION TO RIGHT THOSE WRONGS.

MITO... ?
IT'S MITO-KÔMON!!
ひゃっほーい!!
BOYOING

HA HA HA
カッカッカッ
YÛKO SAYS THAT THE FIRST GUY WHO PLAYED KÔMON-SAMA IS THE BEST!!
I'VE BEEN WONDERING THIS FOR A WHILE, BUT... WHAT IS THAT THING?
WHY WOULD A MANJU STEAMED BUN SPEAK?
B-BMP B-BMP

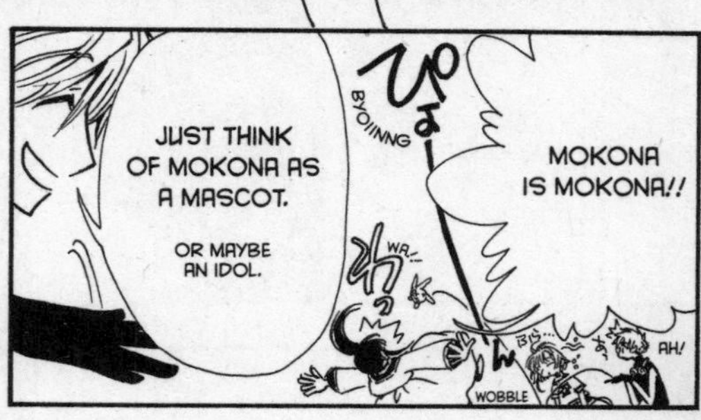
MOKONA IS MOKONA!!
ぴょーん
BYOIINNG
AH!
WOBBLE
WA...!
JUST THINK OF MOKONA AS A MASCOT.
OR MAYBE AN IDOL.

MOKONA'S AN IDOL!
モコナ アイドル
TWRL TWRL
SO YOU THINK WE'RE THIS AMEN'OSA OF YOURS...
UM...
MMMMM!
RUBB RUBB
CHU'NYAN.

春香ちゃんね
CHU'NYAN-CHAN, HUH?
MY NAME'S FAI.
AND...
THIS IS SYAORAN-KUN.
WE HAVE SAKURA-CHAN OVER HERE.
AND FINALLY ...
THIS IS KURO-PUU!
黒ぷー♥
KURO-PUU!
THAT'S "KUROGANE" !!

IN OTHER WORDS...
...FOR YOU TO WISH THAT THIS AMEN'OSA WERE TO COME, YOU MUST THINK THIS LEADER OF YOURS IS A BAD MAN.
HE'S THE WORST!
HE TOOK MY OMONI... MY MOTHER, AND...

IS THAT THE WIND?
KUNK
KUNK
EVERYBODY!
YOU CAN'T GO OUTSIDE!!
WHRRROOO GGHH
RATTL
RATTL
KRA-KAMM

WROOGGHH

AAHH! MOKONA'S GETTING BLOWN AWAY!!
KRAK
KRAK

WHRROOGGH
KRAKK
FSSH
KRAKK

THAT WAS NO NATURAL WIND...
...JUST NOW.

IT'S THE RYANBAN!
GRN
HE'S THE ONE...
...WHO DID IT ALL!!

PAAAAA
KM

FATHER!
ABOJI!
YOU DID IT!
TMP
TMP
YES...

NOW THE TOWN OF RYONFI KNOWS THE POWER OF ITS RYANBAN!
YAY!
BUT WHO DO YOU THINK THOSE PEOPLE ARE?
ABOJI?

THEY COULDN'T REALLY BE AMEN'OSA, COULD THEY?

EVEN IF THEY ARE AMEN'OSA...
AS LONG AS I HAVE THIS, NO ONE CAN OPPOSE ME!

Chapitre.16
Empty Memory

ツバサ
RESERVoir CHRoNiCLE

BAMM
WHY...
...DO I...
KAMM
...HAVE TO...
...WORK ON...
...SOME-BODY ELSE'S HOUSE...
ZAWWZAWWZAWW
KANK KLUNK
...HUH?!
SHE LET US STAY OVER AT HER PLACE LAST NIGHT.
IT'S ONLY NATURAL, ISN'T IT?
GONK
BUT...
A KID LIKE THAT LIVING ON HER OWN...
AND IN THIS HOUSE!
WELL...
CHU'NYAN-CHAN DID SAY THAT HER MOTHER DIED...
するする
ZLLIP ZLLIP
OKAY...
SO HOW LONG DO WE NEED TO STAY HERE?
THAT'S ALL UP TO MOKONA.

あーくそー!
AWW, DAMMIT!
WHY DOES THAT STUPID MANJU BUN HAVE TO BE ON THAT BRAT'S SHOULDER ALL THE TIME?!
とんかんとんかん
BAM BAM BAM BAM
とんかんとんかん
BAM BAM BAM BAM
あははは
HA HA HA HA!
CHU'NYAN-CHAN OFFERED TO TAKE SAKURA-CHAN AND SYAORAN-KUN ON A RECONNAIS-SANCE MISSION.
MOKONA MIGHT BE ABLE TO SENSE SOMETHING.
IS IT ALL RIGHT TO TAKE THE PRINCESS OUT LIKE THIS?
YOU NEVER KNOW IF SHE'S ROWING THE BOAT OR ASLEEP AT THE OAR.

SHE DOESN'T HAVE ENOUGH MEMORIES YET...
...TO RETURN TO THE OLD SAKURA-CHAN AGAIN.
SHE'S ONLY BEEN ABLE TO RETRIEVE TWO FEATHERS.
EVEN THOUGH IT *DOES* SEEM THAT A FEW MEMORIES HAVE RETURNED.

SHE DOESN'T REALLY HAVE HER WILL OR CONSCIOUS-NESS BACK.
NOT THE SAKURA-CHAN WE'RE TRAVELING WITH NOW.
THAT'S WHY WE— TWO GUYS WHO ARE HERE JUST TO TRAVEL BETWEEN WORLDS— CAN'T REALLY OBJECT.
AND...
...EVEN IF SHE GETS ALL HER FEATHERS BACK...
...SHE'LL NEVER BE ABLE TO REMEMBER SYAORAN-KUN.
......

BUT SYAORAN-KUN'S STILL SEARCHING ...
...ISN'T HE?
HE'S GOING TO TRAVEL ALL THE WORLDS AND FIND SAKURA-CHAN'S SCATTERED FRAGMENTS OF MEMORY...

...NO MATTER HOW PAINFUL IT WILL BE FOR HIM IN THE END.

IN ANY CASE, IT'S OUR JOB TO MAKE REPAIRS WHILE WAITING FOR THEM TO COME HOME.
I WONDER IF THEY'LL BRING PRESENTS?

SO...
POPP

DO-DOOOM
HM?
WHERE DOES THAT GIVE YOU THE RIGHT TO RELAX AND DRINK TEA?!
VOOM
おまえもヤレよ!!
GET TO
WORK!!
BOCH
BUT...
...I'M SUPERVISING KURO-PIPPI'S HARD WORK!

DO YOU FEEL A POWER WAVE FROM A FEATHER?
うーん MMMM
うーん MMMM
がっくし SLUMP
MOKONA CAN'T TELL.
The Country of KORYO
THROUGH THIS WHOLE COUNTRY...
...MOKONA FEELS IT FILLED WITH A WEIRD POWER!
"WEIRD POWER"?

HO, CHU'NYAN!
YOU'RE DRAGGING AN OUTSIDER AROUND TOWN, HUH?

THEY'RE GUESTS!
THEY CAME FROM A LONG WAY AWAY!
OHO! TRAVELERS!
WILL YOU JOIN US?
WHAT IS THIS?

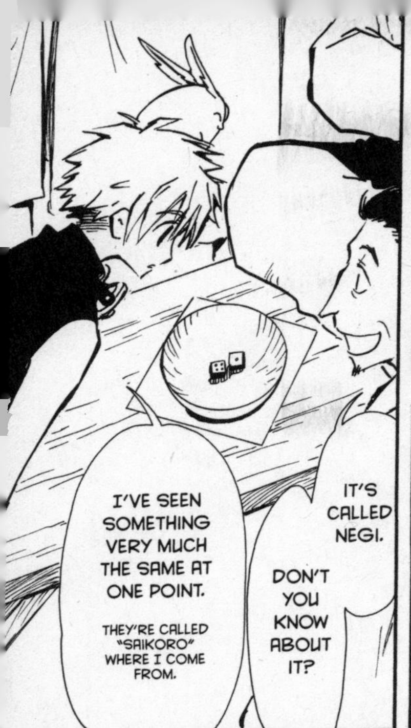
IT'S CALLED NEGI.
DON'T YOU KNOW ABOUT IT?
I'VE SEEN SOMETHING VERY MUCH THE SAME AT ONE POINT.
THEY'RE CALLED "SAIKORO" WHERE I COME FROM.

IT'S EASY!
THROW TWO CUBES.
AND IF THEY ADD UP TO HAVE MORE DOTS THAN YOUR OPPONENT, YOU WIN!

NOW...
...TEST YOUR LUCK!
KLIK
KLAK
THEY JUST LOVE THIS GAME! HONESTLY!
THE OLDER MEN DO, ANYWAY!
WHAT IS THIS?!
MOKONA!!
AAH! IT TALKED!!
THEN... WHO IS THE PERSON WHO THREW THE HIGHEST NUMBER?

I DID! I THREW 11!
BUT...THAT MEANS THE ONLY WAY TO WIN IS TO THROW THE HIGHEST NUMBER ON EACH CUBE, TWO SIXES!
SHE'S NEVER DONE THIS BEFORE!
WHAT KIND OF GAME ARE YOU PLAYING?!
KLKRLL
DADOOOOM
KALAANNG

WAHOO!
SAKURA WON!!
AH... HA HA HA HA
I...I GUESS SOME PEOPLE HAVE THE LUCK.
RUBB RUBB
TIME FOR THE NEXT THROW.
ROLL THEM, YOUNG LADY...
KLAKKLAK
DADOOOM

KLAKKLAK
KLAKKLAK
KLAKKLAK

WAAAAAH!
GIVE ME A BREAK !!

SAKURA WON BIG! ♥
LOOK AT ALL OUR PRESENTS! ♥
WE EVEN GOT CLOTHES!
IS IT REALLY OKAY TO ACCEPT ALL THIS STUFF?
CHOMP
CHOMP
I LOVE PEACH BUNS!
THAT WAS AMAZING!
NO MATTER HOW MANY TIMES YOU ROLLED THEM, THEY CAME UP WITH A PAIR OF SIXES!
YOU MUST BE A FAVORITE OF THE GODS!
MOKONA WANTS THIS!!
"A FAVORITE...
...OF THE GODS"?
SOMEBODY WITH UNUSUALLY GOOD LUCK.
THAT'S WHAT WE CALL THEM!
MY OMONI TOLD ME ABOUT IT!
GOOD LUCK COMES FROM BEING ESPECIALLY LOVED BY ONE OF THE GODS!
I WONDER IF YOU WERE ALWAYS LIKE THAT.
I DON'T KNOW.

WHY NOT?
ALL I REMEMBER ...
...IS MY NAME ...
... AND ...
...SOME PEOPLE FROM A DESERT TOWN.
THAT'S ALL.
THERE WAS DESERT ALL AROUND US...
...BUT THERE WAS A LITTLE BIT OF LOVINGLY TENDED LAND.
THAT'S ABOUT ALL.
BEYOND THAT, I CAN'T REMEMBER A THING.

I'M SORRY.
I DIDN'T MEAN TO ASK ANYTHING SO PAINFUL TO ANSWER.
THE REASON WE'RE TRAVELING NOW IS TO REGAIN MY MEMORIES.
I DON'T KNOW ANYTHING OF IT REALLY...
...BUT HE TOLD ME ALL ABOUT IT.
AHHH!
HIM... UM...
SYAORAN-KUN TOLD ME.
UM... SYAORAN-KUN?
IS IT OKAY IF I CALL YOU JUST "SYAORAN"?

MY BIG BROTHER SAYS...
...THAT IF THERE IS SOMEONE YOU ESPECIALLY LIKE, YOU CAN CALL HIM BY HIS NAME ONLY!
AND SO...
...YOU CAN JUST CALL ME SAKURA!
OKAY?
SYAORAN?
OF COURSE.
YOUR HIGHNESS.

SLAKK
YOUR STORE HASN'T PAID THE RYANBAN'S TAX MONEY, HAS IT?!
DON'T! PLEASE!!
KASHAKK
SWIPP
MY FATHER IS OLD AND SICK! AND A SICK HARABOJI NEEDS HIS MEDICINE!
ALL I ASK IS FOR YOU TO WAIT A LITTLE WHILE LONGER!
NO MORE WAITING!!

YOU WILL PAY ALL OF THE TAXES YOU OWE IN FULL NOW!!
WE CAN'T!
YOU'RE CHARGING TWENTY TIMES WHAT THE OLD RYANBAN CHARGED!
THERE'S NO WAY WE CAN PAY THAT!

ZWIPP
THEN THIS OLD MAN OF YOURS IS GONNA FEEL A LOT MORE OF MY WHIP!
NO!!
100 LASHES!!
TMP
STOP IT!!
FSSHH

DOMM

Y-YOU'RE THE BASTARD...
...FROM YESTERDAY!!

GET OUT OF MY WAY!
GRRRRRRRR
WELL, YOU'RE NOT HIM! YOU'RE JUST HIS SON!!
AND A STUPID ONE AT THAT!
I WILL NOT!
DO YOU REALLY WANT TO KNOW JUST HOW TERRIFYING THE RYANBAN OF RYONFI CAN BE?!

SHUT UP!!
FWUT
I KNOW THAT FAN!!
GO!!
GWHOOOHH

ZWAMM
SWAMM
HE CAME OUT OF A FAN?
THAT WAS MY OMONI'S FAN!
AS A SHINBAN, MY MOTHER COULD USE THE SECRET ARTS!

PEOPLE WOULD ASK HER TO MAKE MEDICINES OR CAST CHARMS.
SHE HAD SOME WONDERFUL POWERS!
BUT SHE WOULD NEVER HAVE USED THAT POWER FOR BAD PURPOSES!
SHE HAD PRIDE IN HER JOB AS A SHINBAN!

BUT THAT CREEP AND HIS FATHER...
THEY WERE JUST WANDERING SHINBAN THAT CAME TO TOWN A YEAR AGO!
THEY DIDN'T HAVE ANY SPECIAL POWERS, BUT SUDDENLY THEY BECAME VERY POWERFUL!
THEN THEY CHASED THE OLD RYANBAN-SAMA AWAY AND SET THEMSELVES UP AS RYANBAN IN HIS PLACE!

MY OMONI FOUGHT THEM TRYING TO STOP THEM.
AND THE RYANBAN MURDERED HER!!
TMP
THOK
THOK
!!

WHAT?!
ZHATS
SLATZ

Chapitre.17
The Source of Magic

SLATZ
WATCH OUT!!
THOK

THOK
THOK
THOK
THOK
THOK
ARRRGH!!
GROGGH
THAKOW

ZLISTS
HE DID IT!!
STMP
STMP
DON'T LET IT GO TO YOUR HEAD!

I KNOW THAT SOUND!
WHO-CHAA
THE WIND IS COMING!
WHRRROOOGGHH
GASP

WHUMP
SYAORAN-KUN!!
PLIP
PLIP
YOU GET IT NOW?!

THIS IS THE POWER OF THE RYANBAN!
HYUUU

YOU HAVE TO CALL FOR YOUR DADDY WHEN YOU'RE LOSING A FIGHT?!
YOU ARE THE WORST EXCUSE FOR A FAMILY I'VE EVER SEEN!

SWP

JUST *SHUT* UP!!

IF YOU DON'T LIKE IT, THEN GO AHEAD AND TRY TO BEAT MY ABOJI, CHU'NYAN!!
BUT YOU CAN'T!
WHY?
BECAUSE YOU CAN'T EVEN *TOUCH* HIM!!
HA
HA HA
HAAA

YAP AWAY ALL YOU WANT!

WHEN THE AMEN'OSA COME, ALL OF THE EVIL THINGS THAT YOU TWO HAVE BEEN DOING WILL BE JUDGED!

THEY'LL NEVER COME!
HEH!

AS PUNISHMENT FOR YOUR RESISTANCE, YOUR TAX IS DOUBLED!
YOU CAN'T—
IF YOU DON'T PAY, YOUR STORE WILL BE CONFISCATED, AND YOU AND THE OLD MAN WILL RECEIVE 300 LASHES!

AHHHH HA HA HA HA HA!
STMP
STMP
SLUMP
GRN
.....
!!
DAMN!!!

THUNK
うーん
HMM?
WELCOME HOME!
HOW DID EVERYTHING GO?
THE FACT THAT I WAS ABLE TO TALK TO KURO-TAN THE WHOLE TIME MEANS THAT YOU MUST HAVE STAYED PRETTY NEARBY.
IS SOMETHING WRONG?
I GUESS SOMETHING *IS* WRONG.

I SEE...
YOU WERE DEFEATED BY THE WIND OF THIS RYANBAN GUY AGAIN.
BUT...
...IF THE RYANBAN IS THIS BAD, WHY HAVEN'T YOU RISEN UP AGAINST HIM?
PWP

WE DID TRY...A NUMBER OF TIMES.
A GREAT NUMBER OF TIMES!
THE RYANBAN'S CASTLE HAS SOME KIND OF MAGIC AROUND IT.
NOBODY WAS ABLE TO GET CLOSE.
BUT WE WERE NEVER ABLE TO SET ONE FINGER ON THE RYANBAN.
なるほどー
THAT MAKES SENSE!
THAT ACCOUNTS FOR THE WEIRD POWER THAT MOKONA SENSED, DOESN'T IT?
WITH ALL OF THE WEIRD POWER AROUND, MOKONA CAN'T TELL IF THERE IS A POWER WAVE FROM THE FEATHER OR NOT.
NOD NOD
WHAT ABOUT THAT SON OF HIS?
HAVE YOU CONSIDERED HOLDING HIM HOSTAGE OR SOMETHING LIKE THAT?
HEH
NOW YOU'RE TALKING! ♥
EHP!
HMP?
BY MY WAY OF THINKING, THAT IDEA IS A LITTLE LATE IN COMING.

WE CAN'T!
THE RYANBAN USES MAGIC TO WATCH EVERY PART OF THE TOWN OF RYONFI!
IF ANYTHING HAPPENS TO THE SON...
JUST LIKE WHAT HAPPENED WITH SYAORAN-KUN YESTERDAY AND TODAY, HM?
うーん
HMMM
YOU'D GET HIT WITH A MAGICAL ATTACK...
YOU SAID THAT THE RYANBAN SUDDENLY GOT STRONGER ABOUT A YEAR AGO...
I WONDER IF THAT HAS ANYTHING TO DO WITH SAKURA'S FEATHERS...

THAT WOULDN'T ADD UP.
IT WAS ONLY A SHORT TIME AGO THAT THE MEMORY FEATHERS WERE SCATTERED THROUGH THE WORLDS.
SSP
WE'RE IN DIFFERENT DIMEN-SIONS.
IT'S POSSIBLE THAT TIME FLOWS DIFFERENTLY IN EACH OF THEM.

I'LL GO CHECK ...
...ON WHETHER THE RYANBAN HAS A FEATHER OR NOT.
GRMP
WAIT!
SYAORAN-KUN, YOU'RE WOUNDED!
I'M FINE!
BUT...

EVERY-THING WILL BE OKAY.
IF THERE'S A FEATHER, I'LL GET IT BACK FOR YOU.
SYAORAN-KUN...

JUST WAIT A MOMENT.

AH, NO...
YOU CAN RELAX.
I'M NOT TRYING TO STOP YOU.
IT'S JUST...

THE MAGIC OF THE RYANBAN IS PRETTY STRONG.
IF YOU SIMPLY WALK THERE, YOU'LL NEVER SUCCEED.
AT THE VERY LEAST, WE'LL NEED ENOUGH POWER TO CREATE AN ENTRANCE TO THAT CASTLE.

CAN'T *YOU* DO SOME-THING ABOUT THAT?
IMPOSSIBLE!
VSSH

MOKONA WILL ASK!!
QUIT PRETENDING YOU HAVE A PLAN WHEN YOU DON'T!!
WHO? THE SPACE-TIME WITCH?

PAAAAAA
AH? MOKONA...
...WHAT'S UP?
IT TALKED!!
YAAAAAAH!!

MOKONA SURE IS CONVENIENT AT TIMES!
WE CAN TALK TO DIFFERENT DIMENSIONS!
THERE ARE LIMITS TO HOW CONVENIENT THINGS SHOULD BE!!
SEE?!

I SEE.
SO YOU HAVE TO BREAK THROUGH THE MAGIC—IF THAT'S WHAT IT IS—TO ENTER THE CASTLE?
THAT'S THE PROBLEM.

WHY WOULD YOU NEED TO CONTACT ME?
FAI CAN USE MAGIC, CAN'T HE?
I TURNED OVER THE SOURCE OF MY MAGIC TO YOU.

THE MARKINGS THAT MADE UP YOUR PAYMENT TO ME...
...WERE A DEVICE THAT HELD YOUR MAGICAL POWER IN CHECK.

YOUR MAGIC NOW IS WHAT IT WAS ORIGINALLY MEANT TO BE.
BE THAT AS IT MAY...
...WITHOUT THOSE MARKINGS, WHO COULD EXPECT YOU TO BE ABLE TO WIELD YOUR MAGIC?
FINE.
I'LL HAND OVER SOME-THING THAT WILL HELP BREAK THE MAGIC ARTS SURROUNDING THE CASTLE.
BUT I'LL EXPECT PAYMENT IN RETURN.

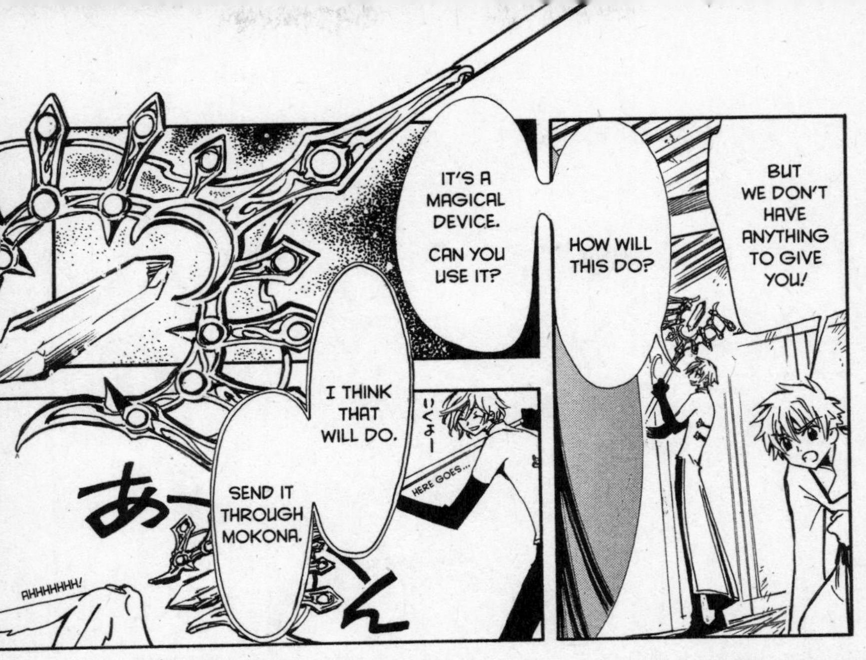
BUT WE DON'T HAVE ANYTHING TO GIVE YOU!
HOW WILL THIS DO?
IT'S A MAGICAL DEVICE.
CAN YOU USE IT?
I THINK THAT WILL DO.
いくよー
HERE GOES...
SEND IT THROUGH MOKONA.
あーん
AHHHHHHH!

ずるずるずる
ZUULUULUULUU
うわー
AAAAAAH!
うわー
AAAAAAAH!

ごっくんっ
GULP
ARE YOU SURE?
YES... I'M SURE.
BOINK

POP
SLOOM
THIS...
...WILL DEFEAT THE CASTLE'S MAGIC?

Chapitre.18
The Castle of Traps

NO!!
I WANT TO GO TO THE RYANBAN'S CASTLE, TOO!
THE RYANBAN'S CASTLE IS PROTECTED BY SOME POWERFUL MAGIC.
THIS IS GOING TO BE DANGER-OUS.
HUMPH
GLANCE GLANCE
BECAUSE YOU'RE SO SHY?
SO SHY! ♥
I'M PREPARED FOR THAT!
I'M GOING!
HMMM.
I'M NOT GETTING THROUGH TO HER.
I DON'T HAVE ANY TALENT FOR EXPLAINING THINGS TO KIDS!
POKK

I'M GOING TO GO AND TAKE DOWN THAT RYANBAN!
I HAVE TO AVENGE MY OMONI!
I'M GOING WITH YOU!
IT'S OKAY, ISN'T IT?
SYAORAN!!

NO.
YOU WILL STAY HERE AND WAIT WITH HER HIGHNESS, PRINCESS SAKURA.
SYAORAN-KUN...

IT'S BECAUSE I'M JUST A KID!
AND I'M NOT MUCH USE WITH MAGIC YET.
HE THINKS I'LL JUST GET IN THE WAY!
THAT ISN'T THE REASON AT ALL.

I THINK YOU SHOULD HAVE SAID IT.
I DON'T HAVE ANY STRONG MAGIC...

THE REASON YOU'RE NOT TAKING CHU'NYAN ALONG...
...IS BECAUSE SHE'S ALREADY SUFFERED TOO MUCH HARDSHIP.

THE RYANBAN SAW THAT SHE TOOK IN STRANGERS LIKE US, AND IF WE BROUGHT HER TO STORM THE CASTLE...
...AND IF FOR SOME REASON WE AREN'T ABLE TO DEFEAT THE RYANBAN, CHU'NYAN WILL SUFFER THE WORST FOR IT.
.....

WHAT-EVER ELSE HAPPENS...
...IT'LL BE BETTER IF WE TAKE THE RYANBAN...
...AND PUT HIM OUT OF OUR MISERY!
HEH

SO...
WHAT HAPPENS IF WE FIND OUT THAT THE RYANBAN DOES HAVE ONE OF SAKURA'S FEATHERS?

I'LL GET IT BACK!

SO, THEY'VE COME.

LET THEM COME!
THOSE FOOLS!
I WONDER WHAT THAT CHILD HAS HIDDEN?
I SENSE A STRONG POWER.

D–
DON'T WORRY, ABOJI!
NO ONE CAN STAND AGAINST YOUR MAGIC!

THAT'S TRUE, OF COURSE.
HERE WE ARE.
NO WASTING TIME!
LET'S GET IN THERE!
GRRN
GRRN
IT'S USELESS TO OPEN THE GATE THAT WAY.
KREEEEE

AAHH!!
WEIRD! WEIRD!
THE CLOUDS ARE BELOW THE GROUND!
CHU'NYAN-CHAN *DID* SAY THAT THE CASTLE WAS PROTECTED BY MAGIC.
YOU'RE TOO IMPATIENT, KURO-MIN!
SHUT UP!
IT WON'T BE JUST THIS GATE.
I IMAGINE THAT ALL OF THE CASTLE GATES WILL BE THE SAME.
SO *THIS*...
VITT

...IS THE TIME FOR THE ITEM GIVEN TO US BY THE SPACE-TIME WITCH.
TA-DAAAAAAH
VOING
YOU THROW IT!!
EH?!
IT LOOKS LIKE A MUDBALL.
HOW'RE WE SUPPOSED TO USE THIS THING?
YOU THROW IT AS HARD AS YOU CAN!
DOOOM
HARD ENOUGH TO HIT THE CASTLE!
AA?
MOKONA, IF I HAVE TO GET IT THAT FAR...
SURE! THAT'LL WORK!
EHEH
WHAT KIND OF PLANS ARE THEY MAKING?

FWOOM
SSLLAA
SLOOLOOLOOM

PASH
BM

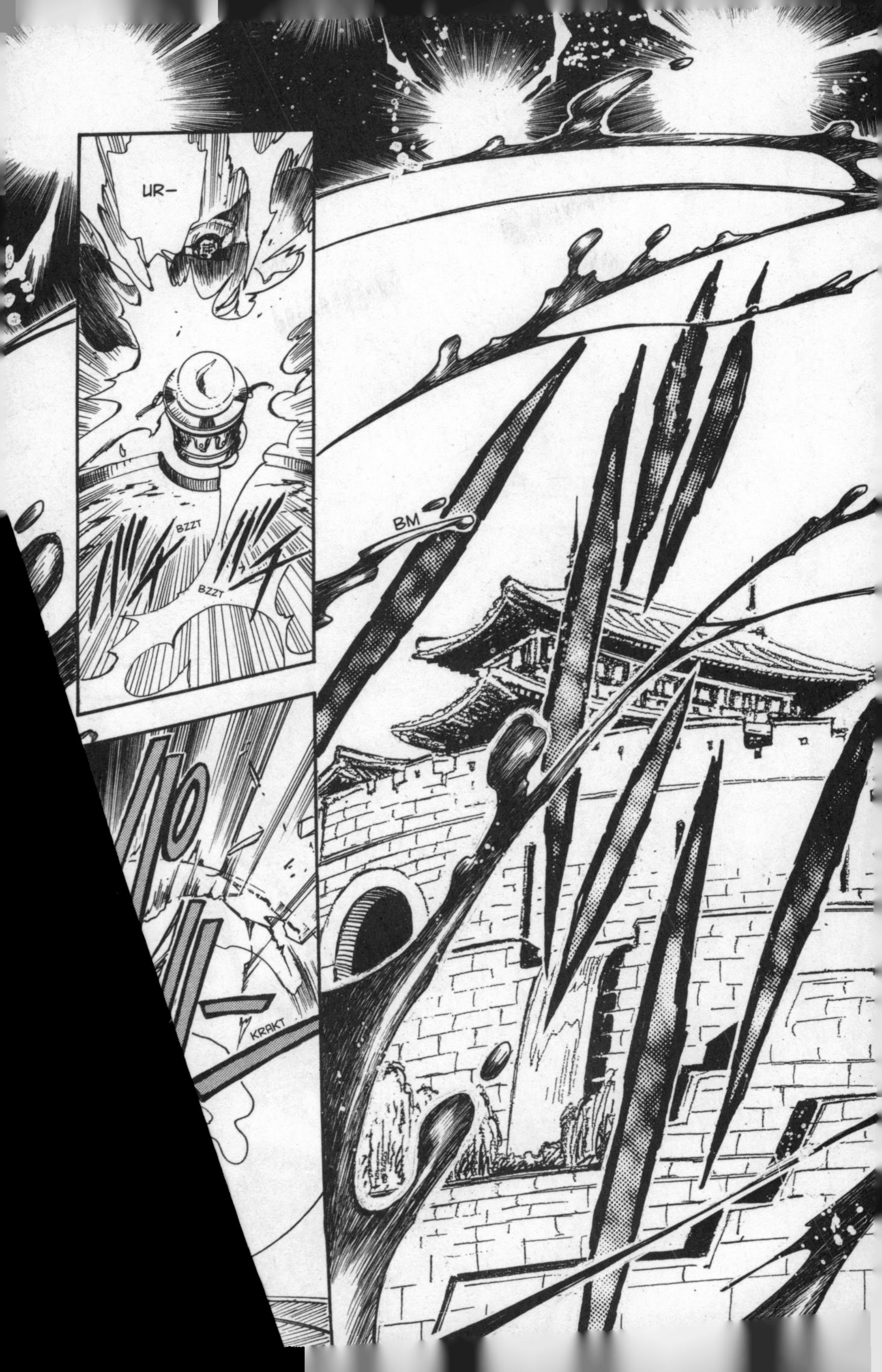
UR–
BZZT
BZZT
KRAKT
BM

PAAA
ABOJI!
THEY'VE BROKEN THROUGH THE MAGIC THAT PROTECTS THE CASTLE!
DON'T PANIC!
MY MAGIC IS JUST GETTING STARTED!
WE'RE WALKING AS FAST AS WE CAN, BUT THE HALL STILL STRETCHES OUT FOREVER.
AND THERE AREN'T ANY DOORS.
KURO-GANE'S LAZY!
WELL, *YOU'RE* ONLY WALKING ON PEOPLE'S HEADS!

WE'RE BACK WHERE WE STARTED.

HM?
I KNOW THIS PLACE LOOKS FAMILIAR, BUT WE NEVER TURNED AROUND!
IT'S BEEN A ONE-WAY TRIP.
I DROPPED THIS ON THE FLOOR AT A SPOT NOT FAR FROM THE ENTRANCE.
WHEET-WHOO!
SYAORAN-KUN, YOU'RE GOOD.
THAT WAS ONE OF THE STONES OF THE GAME THAT FAI AND KUROGANE WERE PLAYING AT CHU'NYAN'S HOUSE!
YOU SAID THE WORDS "WHEET-WHOO." YOU DIDN'T WHISTLE.
I'VE BEEN WONDERING ABOUT THAT.
SORRY, BUT I DON'T KNOW HOW TO WHISTLE.
EH HEH HEH
WHOOO

SO ALL THAT WALKING WAS FOR NOTHING!
IT JUST WEARS YOU OUT!
BUT YOU DIDN'T WALK A STEP!
みよーん
BWAAM
SST
HMM. I CERTAINLY DON'T WANT TO WALK ANY FARTHER.
BOING
.....
IT'S HERE, I THINK.
DID SOME-THING TIP YOU OFF?
FOR THIS KIND OF MAGIC...
...THE PLACE WHERE THE MAGIC IS STRONGEST IS THE SOURCE OF THE POWER.
HM?
I WONDER IF THAT MEANS THE RYANBAN IS RIGHT BEYOND HERE.

I DON'T KNOW FOR SURE.
BUT THERE'S A VERY STRONG MAGIC POWER IN THIS DIRECTION.
I CAN FEEL IT... I THINK.
NOW, KUROGANE-CHI MIGHT BE ABLE TO RELIEVE SOME OF HIS STRESS BY BREAKING THROUGH IT.
たしたしっ
TUMP
TUMP
YOU'RE NOT GONNA USE YOUR GREAT MAGIC POWERS?
I WOULDN'T SO MUCH CALL IT MAGIC.
IT'S MORE LIKE INTUITION.

DO KOWW

BULL'S-EYE!
ガラ
ぴょん
SPROING
KRMBL
KRMBL
KRMBL
SSSHHHH
SOMEBODY'S THERE.

SH-SHK
I WELCOME YOU...
...LITTLE WORMS.

Chapitre.19
The Strongest Kiishim

ABOJI!
THEY FIGURED OUT THE SPELL ON THE HALLWAY!
EXACTLY AS I INTENDED THEM TO.
THAT IS THE STRONGEST KIISHIM IN THE COUNTRY OF KORYO.
SHE KILLED THE FAMOUS SHINBAN, CHU'NYAN'S MOTHER.
THE POWER OF THE FEATHER WAS ABLE TO TRAP HER IN THE CASTLE!
AND THERE ISN'T ANYONE ALIVE WHO CAN OPPOSE HER!

WHO THE HELL ARE YOU?!

YOU HUMANS—PATHETIC CREATURES WITH LIVES SPANNING LESS THAN A HUNDRED YEARS—YOU'RE NO BETTER THAN WORMS!
SUCH CREATURES SHOULD WATCH THEIR TONGUES.
OR SO I SHOULD SCOLD YOU...
...BUT IT'S BEEN SO LONG SINCE I HAD A GUEST, I'LL FORGIVE YOUR COARSE TONE.
WHAT IS SHE SPOUTING?
あ!?
HUH?

WHATEVER!
JUST COUGH UP THE LOCATION OF THAT RYANBAN OF YOURS!
THIS IS SUCH A PAIN!
KURO-BUN, YOUR TEMPER IS A LITTLE *TOO* QUICK HERE!
BOTH SHORT-TEMPERED AND SHY!
THE COMBO'S PRETTY CUTE!

WHAT AMUSING CHILDREN!
TEH HEH
WHAT A NICE COMPLIMENT!
SHE'S CALLING US *KIDS*!!

I THINK THAT SOMETHING I'M SEARCHING FOR IS IN THIS CASTLE.
WILL YOU PLEASE TELL ME WHERE THE RYANBAN IS?
I LIKE THE LOOK IN YOUR EYES.

...I'M AFRAID I CANNOT ANSWER YOUR QUESTION.
HOW-EVER...

NOR...
JINNG
...CAN I ALLOW YOU TO PASS.
SAYING...
EXCUSE ME... ARE YOU SAYING...
...SOMETHING TO THE EFFECT THAT IF WE WERE TO TRY TO PASS YOU, YOU MAY GET...VIOLENT?
EXACTLY.

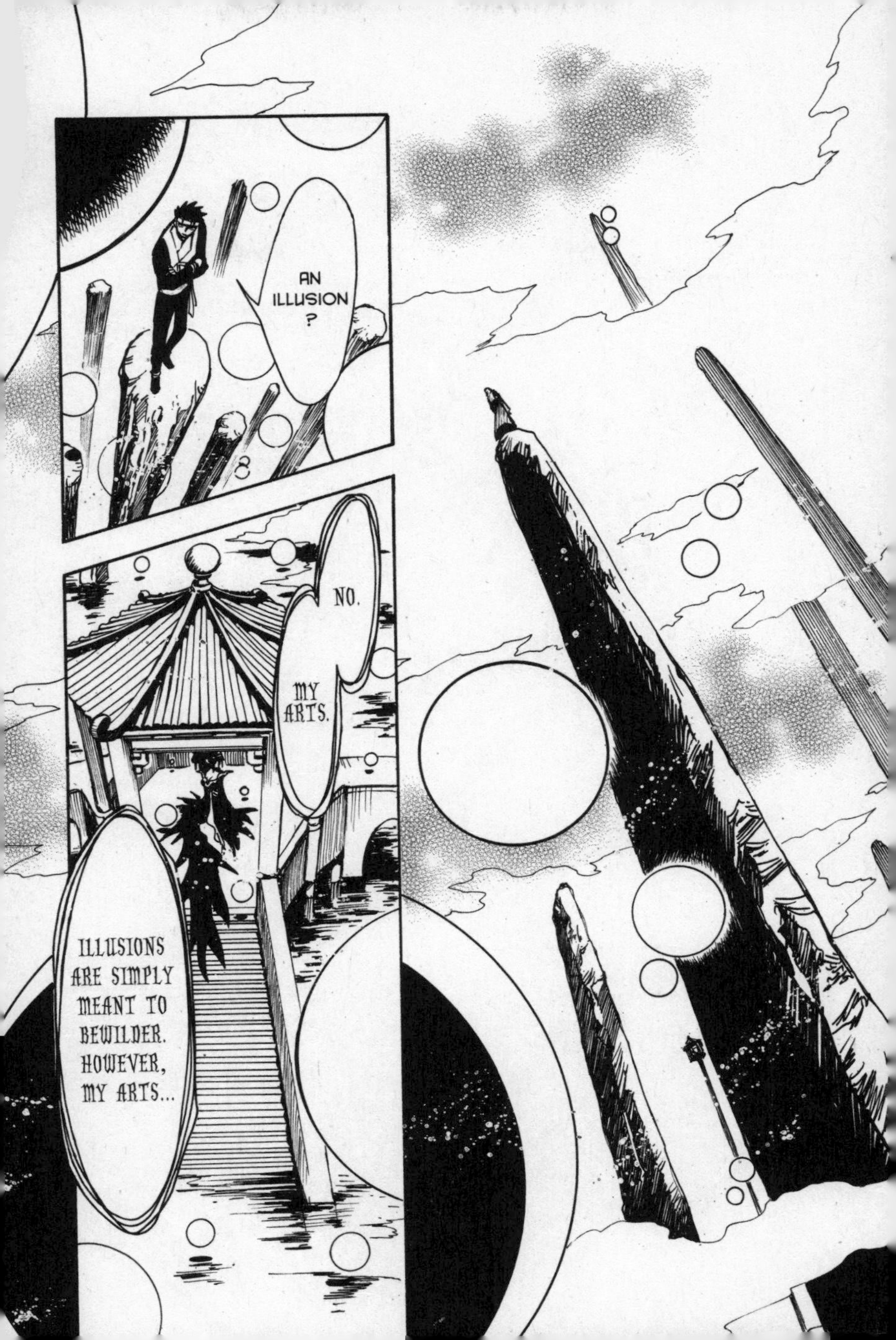
AN ILLUSION ?
NO.
MY ARTS.
ILLUSIONS ARE SIMPLY MEANT TO BEWILDER. HOWEVER, MY ARTS...

ZWIP
...ARE SO MUCH MORE THAN THAT.
PANG
WATER ?!
PLIP
ジュウウウウウウウ
SHHHHHH
..... IT'S MELTING!

ANY INJURIES CAUSED BY MY ARTS ARE PAINFULLY REAL!
SO THAT WOULD MEAN THAT IF WE RECEIVE A SEVERE WOUND...
YOU DIE!
WHOO
OOO

DM
DM
DM
DM
DM
TMP
FSSH
SHOOOM
SSHHHH
!!

UMPH!
WHOOSH
MY LEG!!
SHHHHHHHHH
THE LAKE AND MY SPHERES ARE MADE OF THE SAME LIQUID.
OF COURSE ...
...NOT EVERYTHING YOUR EYE SEES IS AS IT APPEARS.
FSSH
YOU'RE TELLING ME THAT IF I FALL IN THE LAKE, I'M GONNA MELT?!
FSSH

KURO-MIN, BREAK THIS FOR ME.
HUH?
WHY?!
WE WON'T BE ABLE TO AVOID THESE SPHERES EMPTY-HANDED FOREVER!
DO IT YOURSELF!!
KRAKK
PASH
NOW WE CAN DESTROY THE BALLS WITHOUT TOUCHING THEM!

PA
PA
PA
PA
WHEET-WHOO!
KURO-SAMA, YOU'RE WONDERFUL!
VOOM
PASH
VOOM
PASH
I TOLD YOU NOT TO *SAY* THE SOUND!

PASH
NOW...
...WE'LL NEVER GET ANYWHERE PLAYING IN THIS PLAYGROUND.
PASH
VWOO
SYAORAN-KUN...
...TAKE MOKONA AND GO ON AHEAD.
VWOO
WE'RE NOT FINISHED WITH THE BATTLE HERE!
TRUE.
BUT NUMBERS WON'T HELP IN THIS BATTLE.
ALSO...
YOU HAD BETTER MOVE FORWARD WHILE YOUR LEG STILL WORKS.
SYAORAN-KUN, YOU STILL HAVE UNFINISHED BUSINESS, HAVEN'T YOU?

NEVER FEAR!
KURO-PII WILL SAVE THE DAY FOR US!
POFF
ぽん
ME AGAIN?!
THANK YOU!
THE MAGIC IS THINNEST ABOVE US.
SYAORAN-KUN, NO DOUBT YOU'LL BE ABLE TO MAKE IT OUT THAT WAY.

IT'S REALLY HIGH!
SYAORAN, CAN YOU GET THERE?
PUPHEWW
VWIP
AAH! IS *THAT* WHERE THE RUNT WAS HIDING?!
I HAVE A PLAN FOR THAT, TOO!
LISTEN...
I HAVE NO IDEA WHAT YOU ARE JABBERING AMONG YOURSELVES BUT...

...I AM PERILOUS WHEN I AM BORED...
...CHIL-DREN!
SORRY! WE'RE ALMOST FINISHED HERE!
BOW BOW
HERE I GO!
WHY? WHY ME?!
TMP
TUMP

TMP
VWOOM

GRSSH
YOU'RE BOTH SO COOL!
WHEEET!

だから
やめろ
WILL YOU CUT THAT OUT?!
ONE MANAGED TO ESCAPE.
THAT LEAVES ME NO CHOICE.

PAK
PAK
PAK
PAK
SHOOM
I'LL HAVE TO TREAT THE TWO REMAINING CHILDREN WITH MOXIBUS-TION.

I'D SAY OUR SITUATION IS SERIOUS.
...... HUMPH!
HHHHH
SSSHH

ZLIP

SYAORAN!
DOES YOUR FOOT HURT?
IT'S FINE.

IF THAT'S THE CASE...

I'M GONNA HAVE TO MAKE SURE YOU CAN NEVER STAND AGAIN!!
DOOM

Chapitre.20
The Final Battle

ツバサ
RESERVoir CHRoNiCLE

GRRN
RRIPP
RRIPP
ZHAATS
THIS TIME, I'LL BURY YOU...
...WITH MY BARE HANDS!!

THAT'S RIGHT!
MY ABOJI, THE RYANBAN OF RYONFI TOWN AND THE COUNTRY OF KORYO, GAVE ME THIS BODY!

I SENSE THAT WEIRD FEELING FROM HIM REALLY STRONGLY!

THE SECRET ARTS, HUH?

MOKONA, CAN YOU STAY AWAY FOR ME?
WA!
YOU UPSTART LITTLE *BRAT!!*
SYAORAN!
WHOOO

WHOOM

パラ
KRMBL
パラ
KRMBL

SHHHHHH
HHH
YOU WILL NOT BE ABLE TO ESCAPE AS THAT PREVIOUS CHILD DID.
JANGG
TINNG
THIS WATER... HURTS, DOESN'T IT?
THAT'S 'CAUSE WHATEVER IT HITS, IT MELTS.
CLOTHES... SKIN...

FSSH
GLOOG
PRASH
!!

THAK
SPASSH
KURO-MU! YOU'RE MEAN!
KAFF
KAFF
SHHHHHHHH
IF I DIDN'T, YOU'D BE MELTED BY NOW.
I SEE YOUR POINT.
そうなんだけど
NEXT TIME YOU MOVE ME, DO IT WITH A LITTLE MORE CARE, HM?
YOU HAVE SOME SKILL, CHILDREN.
JANNG
BOK
IT'S BEEN ...
BOK

GLMMMMM
...SUCH A LONG TIME...
...SINCE I'VE HAD A WAY TO PASS THE TIME WITHOUT BEING BORED.

KSSH
WHAK
DA-KAK
NN!!
KOK
ZU
HYUUU

!!
GATCH

FOOOM
SYAORAN!!

WHAT IS THIS ?!
IS THIS THE MOST POWER YOU CAN MUSTER?!
IT'S TRUE!
MY ABOJI'S POWER CAN'T BE CHALLENGED!

AWW!
THEY'RE MOVING A LOT FASTER NOW...
BUT WHAT REALLY GETS ME IS HOW THEY CAN CHANGE SIZE!
GWOOOOOO
TSK!
YOU MEAN THE WAY THEY BLOB OUT BIG AND SMALL?
AH HA HA
THAT WOULD BE CHU'NYAN'S MOTHER, I TAKE IT.
THERE WAS ONLY ONE OTHER CHILD WHO HELD OUT AS LONG AS YOU.
A FEMALE SHINBAN FROM THE TOWN OF RYONFI.
SHE DID MENTION A DAUGHTER BY THAT NAME.

PERHAPS WHAT THIS COUNTRY TRULY NEEDS...
...IS NOT THAT FOOLISH RYANBAN AND HIS MEN...
...BUT YOU CHILDREN AND THAT FEMALE SHINBAN.
I HAVEN'T THE ABILITY TO LEAVE.
I MUST LIVE BY THE COMMANDS OF THE LOW-BRED ONE WHO UNJUSTLY CONTROLS MY WILL.

AND ALTHOUGH IT IS A SHAME...
...CHIL-DREN...
JANNG
...NOW IS WHEN WE MUST PART!!
DM
DM
DM
DM

WAH!
HERE IS WHERE I'D SAY IT LOOKS BAD FOR OUR HEROES.
DM
DM
DM
DM
DM
YEAH.
THE MINUTE WE'RE CAUGHT IN THAT, WE'RE DEAD.
UM... THAT DOESN'T WORK FOR ME.
YOU SEE...
...I DON'T DIE VERY EASILY.

I DON'T WANNA DIE EITHER.
LOOK AT WHAT'S HAPPENING!
CAN'T YOU USE A LITTLE MAGIC NOW?
I GOT NOTHING TO DO WITH THIS.
NO.
SORRY.
WHAT NOW, KURO-MI?
I AIN'T DYING HERE.
I GOTTA GO BACK TO MY JAPAN!
GRMP

SH
SH
SH
SH
SH
AND WE'RE NOT GOING ANYWHERE UNTIL THAT WHITE MANJU BUN FINDS THE PRINCESS'S FEATHER, RIGHT?
SO WE'D BETTER STEP IT UP, AND GET TO OUR NEXT WORLD.
PERSONALLY, I DISLIKE STAYING IN ONE PLACE.
WHY'S THAT?
BECAUSE THERE IS A PERSON SLEEPING UNDER-WATER WHO, WHEN HE WAKES UP...
...WILL PROBABLY COME AFTER ME.

SO, I HAVE TO RUN...
...TO AS MANY WORLDS AS I CAN FIND.
......
HAVE YOU FINISHED YOUR FINAL WORDS?
DM DM DM DM DM DM DM
NOW ...
...WHAT DO WE DO?
DESPERATE TIMES... AS THE SAYING GOES.
AH HA HA!
..... HEY!
HMP?

THEN...
.....
FAREWELL.
VWAA

YOU HURRY TO YOUR DEATH?
CHILD?
SSHHAAAAAAA

FFT
WHAT ?!

THWASHH

SYAORAN!
SYAORAN!
GATCH
KYAAA!
RATTL RATTL
WHAT THE HELL IS THIS THING?!
DID YOU CONJURE IT UP WITH MAGIC?!

THE RUMORS...
...TALK ABOUT THERE BEING PEOPLE IN THE AMEN'OSA WHO CAN USE MAGIC!
KYAA!
KYAA!
BUT YOU GUYS DON'T REALLY CALL YOURSELVES AMEN'OSA, DO YOU?

THAKK
FWOOM
THEN I'D BETTER END YOUR NOISE RIGHT HERE!
STOP IT.

FSSH
GRNCH
THE KIISHIM ...
...WOUNDED YOU IN THIS FOOT, DIDN'T SHE?

WELL?
DOES IT HURT?!
GRND
GRND
IS IT AGONIZING?

YOU LIKE TO USE KICKS WHEN YOU FIGHT.
YOU AREN'T GONNA BEAT SOMEBODY AS GOOD AS I AM PUTTING UP A WOUNDED LEG AS YOUR GUARD.
IT ISN'T THERE AS GUARD.

WHAT WAS THAT?!
I DON'T CARE WHERE I'M INJURED.
IT MAKES NO DIFFERENCE.
TWRRR
WHEN I DECIDE TO DO SOMETHING, I DO IT!

KOOOM

AND THAT'S ALL!

YOU'RE QUITE THE...
... LITTLE TACTICIAN, AREN'T YOU?
STABB
HEHN
I JUST DON'T LIKE RAIN.
AND SO...

VYUU
TURN IT OFF!
PATCCH
FYUU

KRAKL
GRR...
THE KIISHIM SHOULD *NEVER* HAVE BEEN DEFEATED!
SNAP
MY SON...
HE SHOULD BE FINISHING UP HIS JOB BY NOW...
FWAA

CHAKL
YOU LITTLE ...
YOU WON'T GET OUT ALIVE !!
VASH

JANNG
IF YOU TRY ANY MORE OF YOUR WEIRD TRICKS...
WHAT KIND OF MAGIC ARE YOU TRYING ON ME NOW?!
THAT WAS A THANK YOU.
INSIDE THAT STONE WERE THE MAGICS THAT KEPT ME IN THRALL TO THE RYANBAN.

あーなるほど
OH! I SEE.
AND WHEN KURO-PON SMASHED THE STONE...
I WAS FINALLY SET FREE.
HAD I THE CHOICE, I WOULD NEVER HAVE DEFENDED THAT BRAINLESS RYANBAN AND HIS SON AGAINST TWO SUCH STEADFAST CHILDREN.

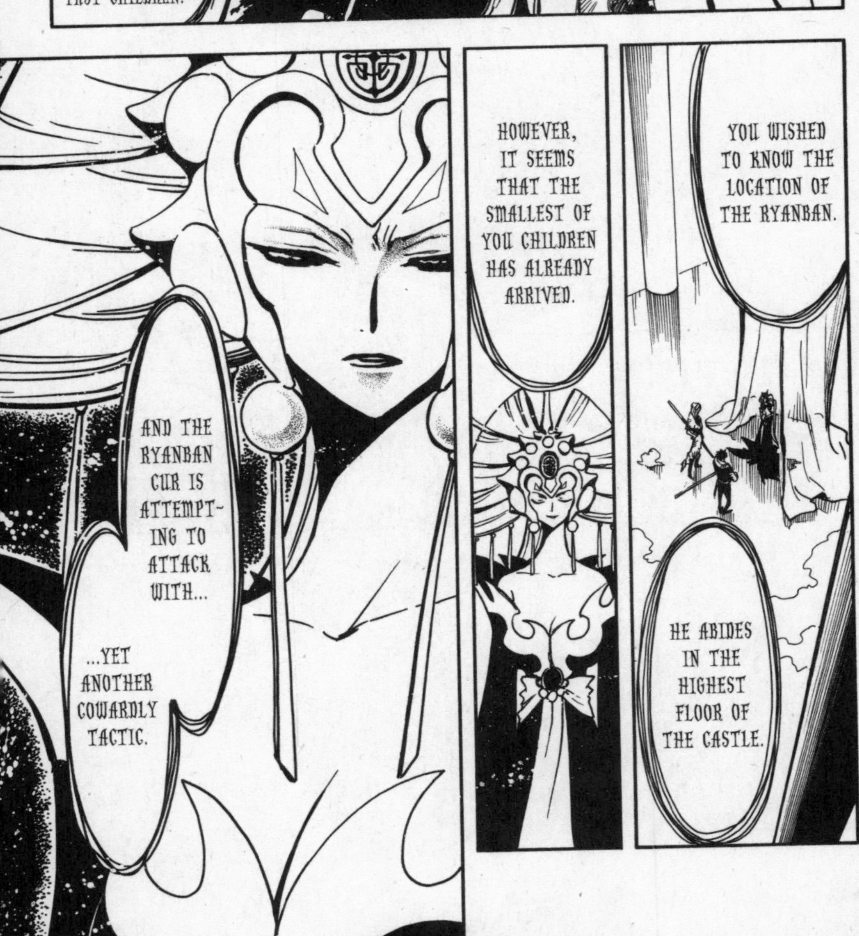
YOU WISHED TO KNOW THE LOCATION OF THE RYANBAN.
HE ABIDES IN THE HIGHEST FLOOR OF THE CASTLE.
HOWEVER, IT SEEMS THAT THE SMALLEST OF YOU CHILDREN HAS ALREADY ARRIVED.
AND THE RYANBAN CUR IS ATTEMPTING TO ATTACK WITH...
...YET ANOTHER COWARDLY TACTIC.

ARE YOU HERE ...
... MOKONA ?
YEAH ...
THIS IS WHERE THE WEIRD POWER IS STRONGEST.
BUT MOKONA'S FEELING REALLY DIZZY...
KREEEEEEE

SAKURA !!
CHU'NYAN !!

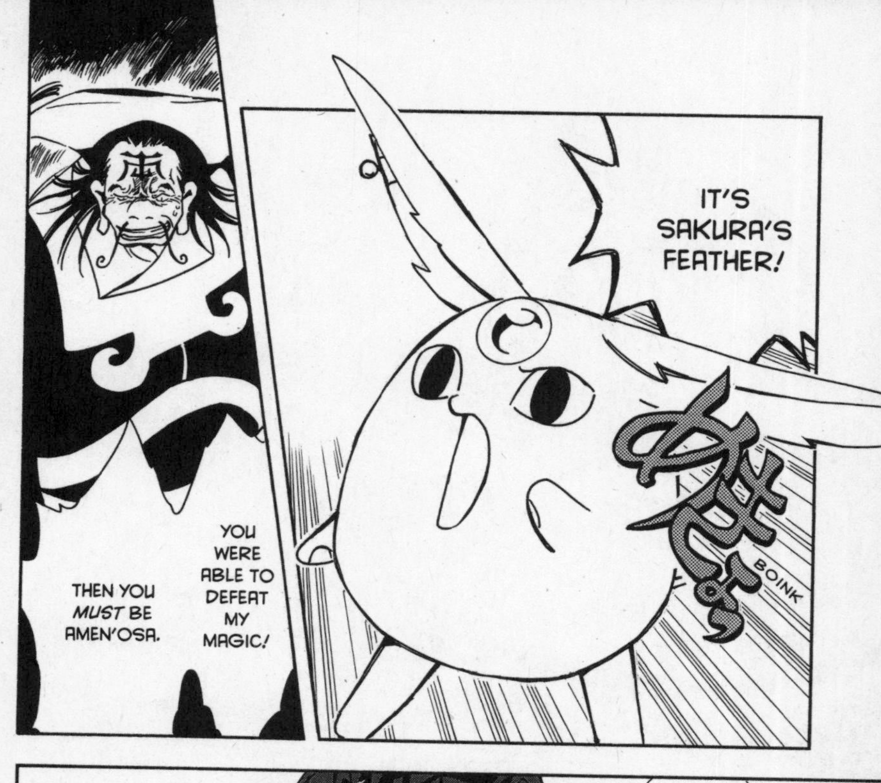
IT'S SAKURA'S FEATHER!
BOINK
YOU WERE ABLE TO DEFEAT MY MAGIC!
THEN YOU *MUST* BE AMEN'OSA.

..... LET THEM DOWN.

SO THEY TOLD THE CENTRAL GOVERN-MENT ABOUT ME.
WAIT...
EVEN IF THEY DID, THERE'S STILL A GOOD CHANCE THAT I CAN DEFEAT AMEN'OSA, TOO.

THWAM
LET THE TWO OF THEM *DOWN!!*

チカッ
CHIKK
VWAKK
SYAORAN!!
JUST SET A FINGER ON ME...
...AND YOU'VE CONDEMNED THEM TO DEATH!!
WHOOSH

TRMBL
FWAAA
SHK
SHK
SHK
SHK
SHK
SHK

THESE ARE THE TOWNS-MEN.
THEY'RE ALL UNDER MY CONTROL.
CAN YOU GET THROUGH THEM TO ATTACK ME...
...BRAT ?!

Chapitre.21
The Mirror of the
Greatest Love

SHAKK
SHAKK
IF YOU ATTACK THESE TOWNS-MEN...
...YOUR TWO YOUNG WOMEN WILL FEEL THEIR PAIN MANY TIMES OVER!!
WHOOSH

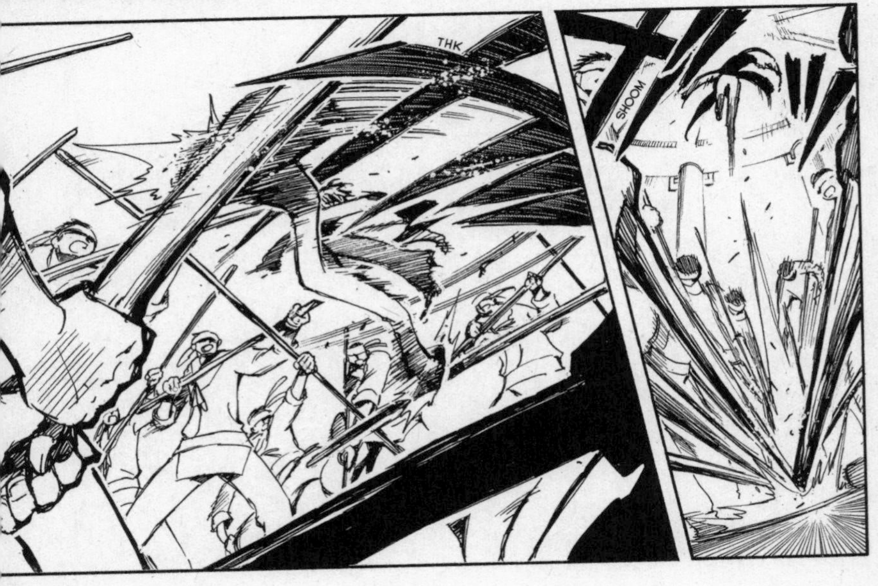
THK
SHOOM

TMP
JUST TRY TO ATTACK THEM, BRAT!
TM
TM
TM
SKREECH
HYAA
WOBBL

WHAT'S THE MATTER?
IS IT OVER ALREADY?!
KRA KOW
SYAORAN!!

WHAK
THOK
SYAORAN!!
HEHN

YES!
AS LONG AS I HAVE THIS FEATHER...
HAAA HA HA
HA HA HA
...NO ONE CAN DEFEAT ME!!

KAK
KAK
KAK
SOME-ONE SAVE HIM!
SAVE HIM...
SYAORAN!!!
PACH

THAT'S JUST A TRICK, TOO?

WHAT WAS THAT?

YOUR HOSTAGES UP THERE ARE JUST FAKES, AREN'T THEY?

WH—
WHAT ARE YOU SAYING?
THEY'RE THE TRUE—
HER HIGH-NESS ...

DOESN'T CALL ME "SYAORAN."

DMP
!!
VWAKK
HYUUN

PK KK

FFF
AH!
PLAYTIME IS OVER.
KRA-KOW

SHMP
AND NOW, MEN...
...IT'S TIME TO END THE BRAT'S LIFE!

EVERYBODY!
FASH
WAKE UP!!

SHAAAAAAAA!
HUH?
WHAT?!
WHAT ARE WE DOING HERE?
THIS MIRROR REMOVES MAGIC CAST ON PEOPLE.
IT WAS ONE OF MY OMONI'S MAGIC ITEMS!
CHATTR
CHATTR
DMM
CHU'NYAN!!
SAKURA TOO!!
POP
AAAAH!

MY ABILITY TO USE MAGICAL POWER MAY STILL BE WEAK...
BUT...
CHAKI

I *AM* STRONG ENOUGH TO USE THIS MIRROR ...
...AND MAKE SURE YOU *NEVER* USE THE TOWNS-PEOPLE AGAIN!
DAMN YOU !!

WHAT'S THIS?
IT SEEMS PRETTY CROWDED IN THERE.

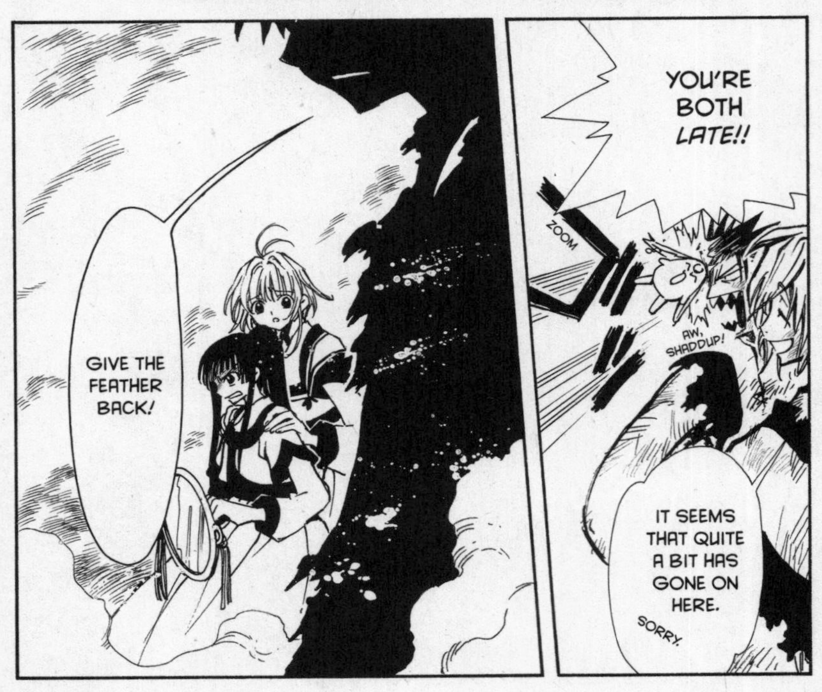
YOU'RE BOTH LATE!!
ZOOM
AW, SHADDUP!
IT SEEMS THAT QUITE A BIT HAS GONE ON HERE.
SORRY.
GIVE THE FEATHER BACK!

YOU MURDERED HER, RIGHT?
YOU'RE THE ONE WHO MURDERED A WOMAN WHO WAS JUST TRYING TO PROTECT THE VILLAGE!!
AND MY OMONI SAID...
...NO MATTER HOW MUCH POWER YOU HAVE...
...YOU CAN'T BRING THE DEAD BACK TO LIFE!!
NO MATTER HOW MUCH I WANT TO BE WITH HER, I WILL NEVER SEE MY OMONI AGAIN!!

AND STILL...
...HE SPOUTS SUCH LIES!!

CHU'NYAN...
DO YOU WANT TO TAKE YOUR REVENGE NOW?

IF IT WILL HELP, YOU CAN TAKE IT.
BUT...
...IS HE REALLY WORTH YOUR EFFORT?
THAT FREAK...
...ISN'T WORTH THE ENERGY IT TAKES TO HIT HIM!

TAK
TAK
D—
DON'T TOUCH ME!
S—
STAY AWAY!!
THAT WILL BE ENOUGH.
ZLOOP

To Be Continued

Translation Notes

Japanese is a tricky language for most Westerners, and translation is often more art than science. For your edification and reading pleasure, here are notes on some of the places where we could have gone in a different direction in our translation of the work, or where a Japanese cultural reference is used.

Tora-Cola

If you will remember from the previous volume, "Tora" means Tiger—the mascot of Osaka's baseball team, the Hanshin Tigers, and the symbol of the entire Hanshin Republic. History buffs might also recognize "Tora" as the Japanese Navy's signal to start the attack on Pearl Harbor: "Tora Tora Tora."

Chu'nyan

What's with the apostrophe? It's just to note that the *n* belongs with "nyan" rather than with "Chu." By the way, "chu" uses the kanji (the Japanese system of writing) for "spring," and "nyan" uses the kanji for "scent."

Ryanban

The "Ry" combination is one of the most difficult combination of sounds for native, monolingual English speakers to wrap their lips around. Many would pronounce "Ryan" as if they were saying the first name of Ryan O'Neal. Not quite. First, remember that the "r"

sound in Japanese sounds like a very light "d" sound—similar to the "r" sound that an upper-class British person would use to pronounce the word "very." Add that to a "ya" sound, and you get a single syllable that sounds a little like "dya." Remember, it's not "di-ya" or "ri-ya," but "rya."

Manju

The same type of big, white, wheat-dough bun as Siu Bao found in dim sum restaurants, and sometimes sold steaming hot on a chilly autumn day by street vendors in Yokohama's Chinatown. Mmmm.

Mito Kômon

One of Japan's most popular hour-long TV dramas, "Mito Kômon" began its run in 1970 and continues today. The main character is an elderly aristocrat who travels Japan with his three retainers, finding injustice and doing what he can to correct it. In the last act of every show, just when the bad guys seem to have the upper hand (reportedly at exactly the same minute mark of every program), Mito-sama pulls out the emblem of his nephew, the Shogun! The bad guys realize that Mito-sama's influence trumps any power they might have, and they capitulate. Like James Bond, the title character has been played by a number of different actors.

Rowing the Boat or Asleep at the Oar

Actually, both of these phrases mean the same thing . . . that Sakura is basically asleep. "Asleep at the oar" is obvious, but "rowing the boat" also means that she's a little brain-numb—probably because of the less-than-towering amount of brain work it takes to row.

Gambling Prizes

Cash payoffs for gambling are illegal in Japan, so you will find that gambling for prizes is a very normal occurrence. Unlike skeeball-style amusement centers in the U.S., the prize counters at pachinko parlors are more like mini convenience stores with food, cigarettes, and household items. In Chu'nyan's country the prizes are a natural product of the barter system, and bringing home groceries from your lucky gambling trip is very common to Japanese readers.

Moxibustion

An ancient Chinese remedy, possibly even the precursor to acupuncture, since the Chinese word for acupuncture literally means "acupuncture-moxibustion." A lit and smoldering stick of mugwort is placed on or over an acupuncture point (sometimes to the point of scarring the skin). When combined with acupuncture, the lit mugwort is attached to heat the needle. Like most Chinese medicine, the purpose of moxibustion is to enhance the blood flow and elevate the chi. The Kiishim intends to treat Kurogane and Fai with a full-body acid-based moxibustion, which would almost assuredly be . . . unpleasant.

Mirrors

Mirrors are a traditional mystic element of the earliest parts of Japanese culture. According to the Kojiki (the book of Japanese myths), the Sun Goddess Amaterasu ordered her grandson, Ninigi-no-Mikoto, to go to Earth, and with him she sent three sacred objects: a magatama (a beadlike jewel accessory), a sword, and a mirror. Those three objects have been passed down in the Japanese imperial family. Mystical mirrors have also crept into Japan's fox-spirit tales and other traditional stories.